Bedfordshire Clangers and Lardy Cake

Traditional Foods from the South and South East

Bedfordshire Clangers and Lardy Cake

Traditional Foods from the South and South-East

Laura Mason and Catherine Brown
Foreword by Hugh Fearnley-Whittingstall

Harper Press
An imprint of HarperCollins*Publishers*

Harper*Press*
An imprint of HarperCollins*Publishers*
77–85 Fulham Palace Road
Hammersmith, London W6 8JB
www.harpercollins.co.uk

Published by Harper Press in 2007

First published in Great Britain in 1999
as part of *Traditional Foods of Britain*
by Prospect Books
Allaleigh House, Blackawton, Totnes, Devon TQ9 7DL
Copyright © 1999, 2004, edition and arrangement, Prospect Books
Copyright © 1999, text, GEIE/Euroterroirs, Paris

Subsequently published by Harper*Press* in 2006 as part of *The Taste of Britain*
Original design by 'OMEDESIGN
Copyright © 2007, edition and arrangement, Harper*Press*
Copyright © 2007, Foreword, Hugh Fearnley-Whittingstall
Copyright © 2007, Preface, Laura Mason and Catherine Brown
Copyright © contributions on p.16/28-9 individual authors
(see Acknowledgements)

This edition produced for The Book People Ltd.,
Hall Wood Avenue, Haydock, St. Helens, WA11 9UL.

9 8 7 6 5 4 3 2 1

A catalogue record for this book
is available from the British Library

ISBN: 978-0-00-779-843-8

Design by Envy Design Ltd

Printed and bound in China

Bedfordshire Clangers and Lardy Cake is part of a series of books about regional British food which include:

From Bath Chaps to Bara Brith
The Taste of South West Britain

From Norfolk Knobs to Fidget Pie
Foods from the Heart of England and East Anglia

From Eccles Cake to Hawkshead Wig
A Celebration of Northern Food

From Petticoat Tails to Arbroath Smokies
Traditional Foods of Scotland

These books originally formed part of the complete volume, *The Taste of Britain*, published by HarperPress in 2006.

Contents

Foreword

Much is made these days of British food culture. Chefs and food writers, myself included, are keen to tell you that it's thriving, it should be celebrated, it's as good as anything our Continental cousins enjoy. Yet sometimes it seems as if our words come rolling back to us, as if bouncing off some distant landmass, unheard and unheeded along the way, so that we begin to have trouble persuading ourselves, let alone others, that there is something here worth fighting for.

The fact is that if you spend much time in supermarkets, or amongst the proliferation of branded fast foods on any high street, or if you eat in any but a handful of UK restaurants or pubs, then the concept of regional British food can seem a bit like Father Christmas, or Nirvana. A lovely romantic idea, but it doesn't really exist, does it?

Well, yes, it does. And if you're having trouble finding it, it may just be because you are looking in the wrong place. The problem, in part at least, is that the best, most uplifting stories about British food culture are being drowned out by the cacophony of mediocrity, and worse. The Turkey Twizzler is front page news – and rightly so, when it is making pre-basted, additive-laced butterballs of our children themselves. Shavings of Turkey 'ham' – 98 per cent fat free, of course – are filling the sandwiches of figure-conscious office workers the length and breadth of the nation. But the Norfolk Black, a real turkey slow-grown and bred for flavour, is out there, too – waiting to show you what he's worth. He's not making a song and dance – just gobbling quietly to himself. Track him down, and you're in for a revelation.

That's why this series of books are so timely, so necessary – and so brilliantly useful. They are a map, an investigative tool that will enable you to leave behind the homogenous and the bland, and set off on an

exciting journey to find Britain's edible treasure – some of which may turn out to be hidden on your very doorstep.

I urge you not merely to browse them, but to use them. Because if you can get out there and discover for yourself some of our great British specialities – whether it's traditional sage Derby cheese, or the Yorkshire teacakes known as Fat Rascals, or a properly aged Suffolk cider vinegar – then you will discover, or at least remind yourself, that food can be so much more than fuel. That it can, several times a day, every day of our lives, relax us, stimulate us, and give us pleasure.

The foods described in this book can all work that small daily miracle of exciting our passions. Not all of them, for all of us. But each of them for some of us. They have been made and honed over generations – sometimes centuries – and they are still with us because enough of us – sometimes only just enough of us – love them. Of course, in many instances, we have yet to discover whether we love them or not. And that is why this book is so loaded with fantastic potential. Everybody has a new favourite food waiting for them in the pages ahead.

I've travelled fairly widely, if somewhat randomly, around Britain, and tracking down and tasting local foods has become an increasing priority for me. Very uplifting it is, too. Approach our regional food culture with a true sense of curiosity, and you can never become an old hand, or a jaded palate. I still feel a great sense of excitement and discovery when I finally get to eat a classic local dish on its own home turf. You can't easily deconstruct the magic formula of a well-made Lancashire Hot Pot, or a Dorset apple cake. It is in the nature of such dishes that their sum is greater than their parts. But you can, when you find a version that hits the spot, instantly appreciate how such dishes have survived the harsh natural selection of public taste, and come to delight, comfort and sustain families and groups of friends for so long.

Recently, for instance, I managed to track down my very first proper Yorkshire curd tart, its delectable filling made from colostrum – the very rich milk produced by a cow for her newborn calf. It was baked for me by a farmer's wife at home in her own kitchen, using the method passed down to her through her family, and it was wonderful – very rich, curdy and slightly crumbly – having a hint of cakiness without the flouriness (I told you deconstruction was a vain enterprise). Anyway, it was a world away from any 'regular' custard tart I'd tried before. What I learnt from that experience, and from many similar ones, is that regionality really does matter. If that tart had been made in Dorset or in the Highlands, it wouldn't have tasted the same. And if it had not been made at all, the world – and on that drizzly autumn day, me – would have been the poorer for it.

There are so many factors that affect the way a food turns out. Cheese is the best example. I love cheese – 'milk's leap toward immortality' as someone once said – and it never ceases to amaze me. It's made from milk, of course, plus something that will make the milk curdle (usually rennet, but sometimes quirkier coagulants, like nettle juice). Two basic ingredients. Yet cheese is one of the most diverse foods known to man. There are hundreds of varieties in the British Isles alone – and a bowlful of fresh, pillowy Scottish crowdie differs so greatly from a nutty Somerset cheddar that it's hard to believe they're basically the same stuff. The breed of cattle and their diet, the local water and pasture, the yeasts and bacteria that live locally in the air, the techniques used to curdle the milk, the way the cheese is pressed, turned, and aged – all these things affect the outcome.

That's why it seems absolutely right to me that only cheese made in a handful of Midlands dairies can be called Stilton, and that beer brewed with the gypsum-rich water in Burton-upon-Trent is labelled as such. What's more, if you understand why regional products are unique – that it's high temperatures and seaweed fertiliser that make Jersey Royals taste different to any other potatoes, for instance – then you know more about food in general. An understanding of regional diversity can only make us more intelligent and appreciative eaters.

This understanding is not always easy to come by. Most other European countries have long taken for granted that local foods should be protected, their unique identity preserved. Hence the French

AOC and the Italian DOC systems. But it's an idea not everyone in this country is comfortable with. I put this down to two things, and the first is the creeping curse of supermarket culture. The big multiple retailers try to tell us that we can eat whatever we want, whenever we want and indeed wherever we want. If you understand the seasonal nature of fresh produce, you know this is neither true nor desirable – and the same goes for regionality. You might not be able to buy genuine Arbroath smokies in every shop in the land, but that is precisely what makes them special when you do find them.

The second reason for resistance to regional labelling is illustrated by the pork pie issue. The pie makers of Melton Mowbray are currently battling to have their product awarded PGI (Protected Geographic Indication) status. That would mean only pies made in the area, to a traditional recipe, could carry the name. Other pork pie makers, from other areas, object to this. They want to call their products Melton Mowbray pies, too, arguing that their recipe is much the same. That's nonsense, of course: a recipe is only the beginning of a dish, a mere framework. The where, the how and the who of its making are just as important. But why would you even want to call your pie a Mowbray pie if it comes from London, or Swansea? Only, perhaps, if you know the real Mowbray pies taste better, and you can't be bothered to make your own recipe good enough to compete.

All of which goes to show why the issue of regionality is as relevant today as it ever has been. It's important not to see *From Bedfordshire Clangers and Lardy Cake* as a history book, a compendium of nostalgic culinary whimsy. The food included here is alive and well, and there is nothing described in these pages that you can't eat today, as long as you go to the right place. That's perhaps the most important criterion for inclusion because our regional food traditions are just as much part of the future as the past. At least, they had better be, or we will be in serious trouble.

The implications for our health, and the health of our environment, are far-reaching. If we eat, say, fruit that's produced locally, not only do we reduce the food miles that are wrecking our climate, but that fruit will be fresher and richer in nutrients. If we can go to a butcher's shop to buy meat that's been raised nearby, we can ask the butcher how it was farmed, and how it was slaughtered. And perhaps we can take our children with us, so they learn something too. In the end, a local food culture, supplied in the main by contiguous communities, militates against secrecy, adulteration – cruelty even – and in favour of transparency, accountability and good practice. What could be more reassuring than knowing the names and addresses of the people who produce your food?

I don't think it's overstating the case, either, to say that a knowledge of regional cooking promotes resourcefulness and a renewed respect for food in all of us. Regional dishes are, by their very nature, simple things. This is folk cooking – a 'nose to tail' approach that uses whatever's available and makes it go as far as possible. For a while now – since conspicuous consumption has become practically an end in itself – our predecessors' abhorrence of throwing away anything may have seemed at best, quaint, at worst, laughable. But as we begin to come to terms with the consequences of our 'have it all now' culture, it is becoming clear that ethical production, good husbandry, environmental responsibility and kitchen thrift all go hand in hand. The frugal culture that gave birth to chitterlings and lardy cake, Bath chaps and bread pudding is something we should be proud to belong to. To re-embrace it can only do us good.

Aside from their currency, the foods in this book have had to prove themselves in other ways. They must be unique to a specific region and they must have longevity, having been made or produced for at least 75 years. Finally, they must be, to use a rather ugly word, 'artisanal'. That means that special knowledge and skills are required to make them properly. Which brings me to one crucial element of good food that should never be forgotten: the people who make it. Almost without exception, the brewers, bakers, cooks, farmers and fishermen who produce traditional foods are what you might call 'characters'. This doesn't mean they are yokels caught in a yesteryear time warp. They are people of passion and commitment, intelligence and good humour, and often extraordinary specialist knowledge. And they know more than most of us about the meaning of life.

Not a single one of them goes to work in the morning in order to make lots of money – you certainly don't choose to devote your life to bannock-making in the hope it will furnish you with a swimming pool and a Ferrari. They do it because they believe in it and, ultimately, feel it is worthwhile. In their own quiet and industrious way, they understand just how much is at stake. The future of civilized, communal, respectful life on our islands? It is not preposterous to suggest it. Use your regular custom and generously expressed enthusiasm to support this modest army of dedicated souls, working away in their kitchens, gardens, orchards breweries and smokehouses all over Britain, and you do a great deal more than simply save a cheese, or a beer, for posterity. You help save the next generation from the tyranny of industrial mediocrity.

Amid this talk of pride and principles, it's crucial not to lose sight of the fact that this is food to be enjoyed, celebrated – and shared with friends. Dishes don't survive down the centuries unless they taste good. You may not need much persuasion to try some of the buttery cakes or fabulously fresh fruit and veg described in these pages. But you will perhaps need a sense of adventure to rediscover the charms of some of the entries. Be ready to cast your squeamishness aside and sample some tripe, some tongue, some trotters as well. If the experience of visitors to our River Cottage events here in Dorset is anything to go by, I'm betting you'll be pleasantly surprised. You'll be taking a pig's head home from the butcher's and making your own brawn before you can say, 'Er, not for me, thanks.'

One element of this series of books to be richly savoured is the language. They are written, by Laura Mason and Catherine Brown, without hyperbole, but with a precision and clarity that far better express their authors' underlying passion and purpose. Another thing that makes them a joy to read is their embrace of the regional food vernacular: Dorset knobs, Puggie Buns, Singin' Hinnnies, Black Bullets and Mendip Wallfish are all to be revelled in for their names alone. Indeed, some might be tempted to enjoy them chiefly as a glorious catalogue of eccentricity, a celebration of the cowsheel and the careless gooseberry, of the head cheese and the damson cheese (neither of which are actually cheese) that make British food so charming and idiosyncratic.

But to do so would be to miss out. Now that this book exists, now that it is in your hands, use it to bring about change. It should not be taken as a slice of the past, in aspic, but as a well-stocked store cupboard, with the potential to enrich our future food culture. See it not as a preservation order for British regional foods, but a call to action. Use this book as a guide, not merely to seek out delicious things that you've never tried before, but also to recreate some of them in your own kitchen. Do that and you'll be actively participating in a great food culture that has always been with us, that is often hidden beneath the mass-produced, homogenous, seasonless food we are so frequently offered, but which may yet have a vibrant future.

This book - along with the rest in the series - is a thorough and splendid answer to the question 'What is British food?' Use it well, and it may help to ensure that is still a meaningful question a hundred years from now.

Hugh Fearnley-Whittingstall

Preface

In 1994 we embarked on a mission to describe as many British foods with regional affiliations as we could find. We were part of a Europe-wide project working within a framework – handed down from Brussels – which demanded a link to the *terroir* (soil). In fact the project, named Euroterroir, was more suited to rural southern Europe than industrialized, urbanized Britain. How do you link Yorkshire Relish to the soil? But ultimately we succeeded in writing up some four hundred British entries. And along the way we asked some broader questions – what are our traditional foods? What is the character of British taste?

We've discovered that many rural treasures had survived against the odds. That sometimes foods with traditional or regional affiliations languished unloved. That sometimes British foods, though not always linking directly to the *terroir*, did have other powerful historical influences which made them special, and distinct, from the rest of Europe. No other country in Europe has a history of spicing to match the British.

Yet our homogenized food supply was clearly inflicting a far-reaching loss of local distinctiveness and quality. The idea, inherent in the project, that foods should be the property of a place and its community (*terroir*, in the context of food in France, carries implications of regionality, cultural groupings and the influence of trade and climate), rather than the trademarked possession of an individual or company, was especially alien.

Our initial research complete, we felt confident that either the Ministry of Agriculture or Food from Britain would take up the cause and publish a book based on the work which had taken us two years to complete. Instead, it was a small publisher in Devon (Tom Jaine of

Prospect Books) who kept the flag flying and *Traditional Foods of Britain* was published in 1999. Eight years on, we welcome this series published by HarperCollins.

We also welcome signs of change. Now, there is more awareness of commercial dilution, and dishonest imitation and therefore the need to protect food names, though the application process for producers is slow and difficult. There are certainly more small producers working locally, but they have to cope with numerous barriers. However much they protest otherwise, powerful supermarket central distribution systems and cut-throat pricing polices are not designed to foster local produce. And consumers do not always pause to consider the more subtle and elusive nuances of foods from closer to home.

Of course the ties of regionality do not suit foodstuffs, and in any case should be just one of many avenues open to British farmers and food producers. But it would be good to see more raw local ingredients transformed into distinctive foods since records show their rich variety in the past. Shops and markets bursting with colourful and varied local produce are one of the great pleasures of shopping for food on the continent. They exist because national policies and local custom support them. They should not be impossible in Britain. These books are not an end, but a beginning.

Laura Mason and Catherine Brown 2007

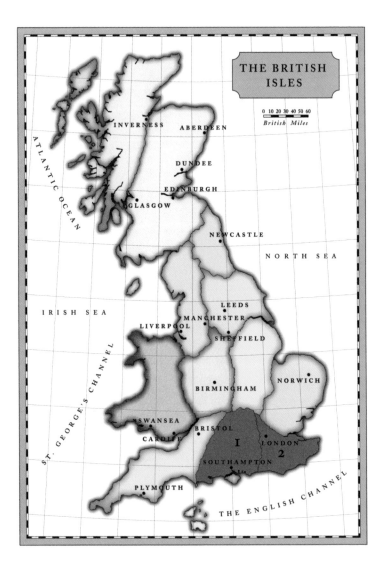

THE BRITISH
ISLES

0 10 20 30 40 50 60
British Miles

ATLANTIC OCEAN

INVERNESS   ABERDEEN

DUNDEE

EDINBURGH

GLASGOW

NEWCASTLE

NORTH SEA

IRISH SEA

LEEDS

MANCHESTER

LIVERPOOL

SHEFFIELD

NORWICH

BIRMINGHAM

ST. GEORGE'S CHANNEL

SWANSEA

BRISTOL

CARDIFF   1   LONDON

SOUTHAMPTON   2

PLYMOUTH

THE ENGLISH CHANNEL

Regions

South England

Blueberry (High Bush)

DESCRIPTION:

BLUEBERRIES ARE SMALL ROUND BERRIES JUST UNDER 1CM DIAMETER; THEY HAVE A THIN BLACK SKIN COVERED IN A POWDERY BLUE BLOOM, GREENISH OR PURPLISH FLESH, AND A DISTINCTIVE SLIGHTLY WINY FLAVOUR.

HISTORY:

High bush blueberries, *Vaccinium corymbosum*, are related to the native British bilberry (*Vaccinium myrtillus*) and flourish in similar conditions. A precedent for the use of blueberries was well established in hill and heathland areas of the British Isles, where the inhabitants were accustomed to using wild blaeberries or bilberries in various sweet dishes. In Scotland, in the hills of Angus and Perthshire, blaeberries were picked by itinerant travellers who used a wooden device which they combed through the small bushes to extract the berries. These they sold in towns and villages to be eaten with cream, used for jam, or made into pies. Since the wild berries are time-consuming to gather, fruit-farmers have been experimenting with the alternative high bush blueberry.

This was developed in New Jersey, USA in 1920, putting to good use acid, boggy soils which had previously been thought worthless for growing. They have been grown in Britain since the 1930s. The first edition of *Law's Grocer's Manual* (*c.* 1895) mentions 'swamp blue-berries', which grew on bushes up to 6 feet (2 metres) high, so it is possible that the British growers were aware of this type of plant some decades earlier but no evidence for their cultivation has been found. According to grower Jeremy Trehane, the bushes with which his family began production were offered free to British growers by a Canadian university in the 1940s. Cultivation has spread to other places in the lowland heath areas of the southern counties of England. In Scotland the berries were originally developed at the Scottish Crop Research Institute at Invergowrie as an alternative to blaeberries.

TECHNIQUE:

High bush blueberries grow well in impoverished acid soils (ideally pH 4.3–4.8, although they can tolerate slightly higher pH if dressed with peat) of the type which underlie many of the heathlands of Britain. The ground is cleared and the bushes planted at an appropriate density. Their only major nutrient requirement is potash, but to do well they do need heathland environments, as good growth relies on the presence of a particular micro-organism in the soil, which is not found in land that has been cultivated. They are pruned lightly in winter to remove old wood which has not fruited in the previous season. Protection from birds is necessary.

REGION OF PRODUCTION:
SOUTH ENGLAND.

Borage

DESCRIPTION:

BORAGE (BORAGO OFFICINALIS) IS A TALL ANNUAL HERB WITH COBALT-BLUE FLOWERS AND STEMS AND LEAVES WHICH ARE COVERED IN COARSE HAIRS; THE LEAVES AND FLOWERS HAVE A FLAVOUR REMINISCENT OF CUCUMBER, AND A NATURALLY COOLING EFFECT WHEN EATEN.

HISTORY:

Borage was probably introduced to Britain by the Romans, and has subsequently spread and naturalized on the chalk hills of southern England. There have been literary references to it since the thirteenth century. It was valued as a medicinal herb, and was made into cordials. Apothecaries considered it promoted cheerfulness and herbalists still use it to ease colds and throat complaints. The herb has also been used to decorate and flavour drinks. Dorothy Hartley (1954) quotes a recipe for claret cup from a Victorian magazine. This gives instructions for each glass to be flavoured with a sprig of borage, commenting on the unique flavour the herb gives and remarking, 'On this account the pretty blue flowers can be had of every gardener during the picnic season, and it is grown under glass all the year round for the express purpose of flavouring claret-cup.'

Borage is grown in gardens on a small scale and produced in larger volumes by market gardeners and specialist herb growers. Several growers who specialize in herbs and salad vegetables, mostly in the southern and eastern part of England, grow borage as part of their mixed crop. Recently, it has been established as a field crop for the sake of the oil that can be extracted. Always recognized as a useful bee-plant, this modern development has allowed some apiarists to produce monofloral borage honey.

The flowers are used to garnish summer drinks, especially Pimm's and claret cups. They are also added alone, or with other edible flowers such as nasturtiums, pot marigolds, chive flowers and heartsease, to salads; the leaves can be added too, if chopped finely. It is also used to flavour vinegars. The seeds can be used for the extraction of oils for food supplements. Until very recently, it was possible to buy borage flowers candied with sugar, although it appears that no-one makes these at present.

Alkanet, a related plant with similar leaves but smaller, rounder flowers is sometimes mistaken for borage; it is edible, although the applications are medicinal rather than culinary.

TECHNIQUE:
Borage is relatively undemanding and although some recommend well-drained calcareous soils, in practice it is tolerant. The plant prefers a sunny aspect. Commercial growers start the plants from seed under glass in about March and plant out in April. Borage is susceptible to frost, and dies back as the weather becomes colder in autumn. Once established, the plants will self-seed and grow again in the same ground year after year. The leaves and flowers wilt easily after

picking, and so are generally picked to order for hotels and restaurants. One technique used by cooks for preserving the flowers is to freeze them in ice cubes.

REGION OF PRODUCTION:
SOUTH ENGLAND; EAST ENGLAND.

Cherry

DESCRIPTION:
ALMOST ALL CHERRIES GROWN IN ENGLAND ARE OF THE SWEET TYPE.

HISTORY:
Wild cherries (geans or mazzards) have been eaten in Britain since prehistoric times (Roach, 1985) but the development of cultivated fruit was the work of Mediterranean cultures. Pliny reported: 'Before the victory of Lucullus in the war against Mithridates ... there were no cherry trees in Italy. Lucullus first imported them from Pontus [Asia Minor] and in 120 years they have crossed the ocean and got as far as Britain.' This seems pretty firm evidence and it is certain that Roman soldiers were plentifully supplied – perhaps from the precursors of the Kentish orchards. In the Middle Ages cherries were a common occupant of garden plots and sold in street markets. However, Europe was still the chief source of the fruit, where climate and skill combined for a larger harvest.

Kent became a centre of cultivation during the sixteenth century, partly because of good water-transport to London, the main market, partly because there were close links with orchardists and gardeners across the Channel. Most varieties grown came from Europe, especially Flanders and France, but there were early signs of specifically English breeds, notably the 'Duke' cherries, hybrids of the sweet *Prunus avium* and the sour *Prunus cerasus*. This group was known to the French as 'Anglais'.

Several classic varieties were bred by nurserymen in the 1800s, including Frogmore Early and Early Rivers, both introduced in the middle of the century. Two others are Bradbourne Black and Merton Glory, the latter introduced in the 1940s. For technical reasons, most orchards consist of several cherry varieties grown together; of the large number of varieties available, about 12 are commercially important.

The area devoted to cherry orchards has sadly diminished and we rely on imports again, as we used to in the fifteenth century, when they were freighted over from Flanders. Kent, however, has kept its first place among the regions of production.

TECHNIQUE:

The custom was to cultivate cherry trees as tall standards with grass underneath. The orchards are grazed by sheep. Most sweet cherries require pollinators and care is needed to choose a compatible variety. Until the twentieth century, geans or wild cherry seedlings from the woods were used as rootstocks. These produce large trees which require very long ladders to gather the fruit; as there is now some reluctance to pick from these, producers have been experimenting with less vigorous rootstocks. The latter have the advantage that they can be netted to protect them from birds during fruiting. A few farms offer pick-your-own facilities for cherry picking.

REGION OF PRODUCTION:

SOUTH AND WEST ENGLAND, KENT, HEREFORD AND WORCESTER, ESSEX, OXFORDSHIRE.

'One must ask children and birds how cherries and strawberries taste.'
JOHANN WOLFGANG VON GOETHE

Cox's Orange Pippin

DESCRIPTION:

A LATE-SEASON DESSERT APPLE, DESCRIBED BY MORGAN & RICHARDS (1993) AS MEDIUM-SIZED (5–7CM DIAMETER) OF ROUND-CONICAL SHAPE, THE BASIN OF MEDIUM WIDTH AND DEPTH, SLIGHTLY RIBBED, WITH RUSSET USUALLY PRESENT; THE EYE SMALL AND HALF-OPEN, THE SEPALS MEDIUM TO LONG AND NARROW; THE CAVITY MEDIUM BROAD, QUITE DEEP, WITH A LITTLE RUSSET; THE STALK OF MEDIUM LENGTH, AND QUITE THIN; THE COLOUR OF THE SKIN CHARACTERISTICALLY DISPLAYING AN ORANGE RED FLUSH WITH RED STRIPES OVER GREENISH YELLOW TURNING TO GOLD, WITH A LITTLE RUSSETING AS DOTS AND PATCHES; WHEN PERFECTLY RIPE, DELICIOUSLY SWEET AND ENTICING WITH RICH INTENSE AROMATIC FLAVOUR; DEEP CREAM FLESH; SPICY, HONEYED, NUTTY, PEAR-LIKE, BUT WITH A SUBTLE BLEND OF GREAT COMPLEXITY.

HISTORY:

The British have concentrated on the development of a uniquely wide spectrum of flavours and qualities in apple varieties; some of the finest are known as pippins. The word originally denoted an apple raised from seed as opposed to multiplied by scions. Morgan & Richards (1993) remark, 'in time the term "pippin" came to be synonymous with fine-flavoured late-keeping English varieties'. From Tudor times, pippins of various types have been popular and commercially important. At first the Golden Pippin was esteemed for making jellies and tarts. Then, the Ribston Pippin (Yorkshire), the Wyken Pippin (Warwickshire) and the Sturmer Pippin (Suffolk) arose, which remained important through the nineteenth century.

The Cox's Orange Pippin was raised by Richard Cox in Buckinghamshire. It is believed to have been grown from a pip of a Ribston Pippin. Commercialization took place in the 1860s in the neighbouring county of Hertford and it was widely planted in southern England over the next 30 years. Roach (1985) illustrates an orchard of Cox's Orange Pippin on dwarfing rootstocks in 1865.

Today, it is the most important British dessert apple. Several clones are grown, including the Queen Cox. As well as being valued for its fruit, the Cox, crossed with other varieties, was the source of various late-season dessert apples, including Ellison's Orange, Epicure, Fortune and Laxton's Superb, several of which are still grown on a small scale.

Other notable varieties classed as late-season dessert types have complex aromatic flavours – sometimes reflected in their names, such as Cornish Gilliflower and Pitmaston Pine Apple (whose honeyed flavour is considered reminiscent of that fruit). These, and many others, were greatly enjoyed by Victorian and Edwardian connoisseurs when fine-flavoured dessert apples were much appreciated by the rich. That wealth of varieties has since reduced as a consequence of the modern emphasis on ease of growth and handling, and the uniform and attractive appearance demanded by supermarkets. However, a renewal of interest in rarities has been prompted by enthusiasts.

Many of these apples are now much grown abroad, including the Cox and the Sturmer. Controlled-atmosphere storage, very important to Cox's and some other late-season apples, has been used in Britain since the 1920s. Cox's Orange Pippin is generally eaten raw, although it can successfully be used in pies, tarts and cooked desserts. Some aromatic dessert apples have been used for single-variety juices.

TECHNIQUE:
See Bramley's Seedling for details about rootstocks. Cox's are not suitable for cultivation in the northern half of England, or in areas of high rainfall. They require free-draining soils, and are mostly concentrated in the south-east of Britain. Optimum pollination time is mid-May; the tree is of medium vigour and is a good cropper, but prone to mildew, scab and canker which are controlled by lime sulphur sprays. For commercial production, the fruit is chemically analysed to determine storage potential; picking is then carried out by hand. Cox's are picked in late September and early October. Grading is by diameter (sizes are set according to variety) and by quality (EU standards, for appearance) into Grade 1 or Grade 2. Storage in

controlled atmosphere (low in oxygen, high in carbon dioxide) and temperature allows Cox's to be kept until spring.

REGION OF PRODUCTION:
SOUTH ENGLAND.

Egremont Russet Apple

DESCRIPTION:

A MID-SEASON DESSERT APPLE. DESCRIBED BY MORGAN & RICHARDS (1993) AS A MEDIUM-SIZED APPLE (5–7CM DIAMETER), FLAT-ROUND IN SHAPE, THE BASIN BROAD AND QUITE DEEP, THE EYE LARGE AND OPEN, THE SEPALS BROAD-BASED, AND QUITE DOWNY; THE CAVITY NARROW AND SHALLOW, LINED WITH RUSSET; THE STALK VERY SHORT AND QUITE THIN; THE COLOUR IS CHARACTERIZED BY OCHRE RUSSET (ROUGH-TEXTURED AREAS OF SKIN) WITH A SLIGHT ORANGE FLUSH ON GOLD GROUND COLOUR; THE FLESH IS CREAM COLOURED AND THE FLAVOUR IS NUTTY, WITH A SMOKY TANNIC DRYNESS DEVELOPING ON KEEPING.

HISTORY:

Russet pippins were described in the seventeenth century. This may simply have indicated red-flushed apples, as the word russet also carries a meaning of redness. Russet in the sense of rough-skinned does not seem to have been used until late in Victoria's reign. It was in the second half of the nineteenth century that the Egremont Russet was first noted. Exactly where it originated is unknown: it was first recorded in Somerset, but the name suggests a link with the estate of Lord Egremont at Petworth (Sussex). The head gardener from the estate maintained that it was raised there (Morgan & Richards, 1993). It was commercialized in the early twentieth century but suffered from being in season at the same time as the Cox's Orange Pippin. However, demand has continued and the Russet is still available.

The enthusiasm of the British for after-dinner drinking of port accompanied by fruit and nuts is one reason for their affection for the russets as a group. Their especial flavour, reminiscent of nuts and spice, and happy balance of sweetness and acidity matched that of the wine far better than any other style of dessert apple.

TECHNIQUE:
See Bramley's Seedling for details about rootstocks. Optimum pollination time for Egremont Russet is early May; the tree is of medium vigour and upright habit, hardy and a good cropper; it is resistant to scab but prone to bitter pit. Picking is by hand in late September and early October. Grading is by diameter (sizes are set according to variety) and by quality (EU standards, for appearance) into Grade 1 or Grade 2. Egremont Russet can be stored for only a short time.

REGION OF PRODUCTION:
SOUTH ENGLAND.

Lord Derby Apple

DESCRIPTION:
A MID-SEASON COOKING APPLE, LARGE, ROUND-CONICAL TO OBLONG-CONICAL, GREEN, WITH SLIGHT PINK OR PURPLE ON CHEEK. FLAVOUR: STRONG, ACID, REQUIRES SUGAR.

HISTORY:
This apple was raised in the mid-nineteenth century in Cheshire, and commercialized shortly afterwards. It is possible that the apple originated from a seedling of the older English cooking variety called, because of its profile, the Catshead. This had been known since the early seventeenth century, and was popular for making dumplings in the 1800s. Unlike the codlin type of cooking apples, Lord Derby keeps its shape when cooked. Other cooking apples in season at this time are the old variety known as Harvey, first recorded in the 1600s, and Stirling Castle, both of which cook to a purée. They are now rare and little grown. Lord Derby is especially good in pies.

TECHNIQUE:
See entry on Cox's Orange Pippin for more details of apple growing.

Samphire

DESCRIPTION:

THE LEAVES OF MARSH SAMPHIRE GROW IN BRIGHT GREEN SPEARS, SOMETIMES DESCRIBED AS LOOKING 'LIKE A BRANCH OF CORAL'. FLAVOUR: VERY SALTY.

ROCK SAMPHIRE IS MORE PINNATE, GROWING ON ROCKY CLIFFS AND SLOPES BY THE COAST.

HISTORY:

There are 2 forms of samphire. The first, and original, is rock samphire (*Crithmum maritimum*). The second is marsh samphire, once more commonly known as glasswort (*Salicornia stricta*) because it was used as a source of soda for glassmaking. Glasswort is found on many tidal marshes around the British coast. It is very common, and best known in Norfolk. Spencer (1994) observes that, unlike rock samphire, which was highly esteemed in the past, marsh samphire was historically a food for the poor. In the late nineteenth century it was a substitute for the increasingly rare rock samphire. Since the second half of the twentieth century, marsh samphire has become better known generally.

Rock samphire still grows abundantly on the coasts of southern Britain. It was the subject of a much-quoted line in *King Lear*, when Edgar wishes to deceive blind Gloucester into thinking he is on the cliffs at Dover: 'Half way down hangs one that gathers samphire, dreadful trade!' he exclaims.

Culpeper the herbalist remarked in 1656 that samphire was not as much used as it was, but the statement was no barrier to a battery of seventeenth- and eighteenth-century recipes, especially for pickles, the form that mostly reached the table. Nor was it in such short supply that it could not be hawked on the streets of London as 'Cress marine!' However, the curious intelligence of John Evelyn (1699) wished to pursue the possibility of cultivating the plant, to assure supplies, much as they did, he observed, in France. His venture was of little success and the plant here has remained obstinately wild. Evelyn included a recipe for pickling samphire 'the Dover way' – it was Mr John Bullen of Dover who sent him his experimental seeds, a descendant, perhaps, of Edgar's labourer.

It is possible that there was insufficient rock samphire to maintain a large-scale trade, or the dangers of clifftop gathering were too fatal, but there are signs at the end of the eighteenth century that supplies were running out and a substitute was needed. Here we might bring forward another poet's reference, John Phillips:

> How from a scraggy rock, whose prominence
> Half overshades the ocean, hardy men
> Fearless of rending winds, and dashing waves,
> Cut samphire, to excite the squeamish gust
> Of pamper'd luxury...

Hugh Smythson in *Compleat Family Physician* (1781) lets fall that it was 'not often brought genuine to London'. The more easily gathered glasswort, already the object of industrial exploitation for the glass trade, was a willing candidate, but it is not entirely clear that its offer, or that of its vendors, was ever taken up. There may have been a plethora of early recipes, but there are few in Victoria's reign, implying an acceptance of the scarcity of the original plant (Tee, 1983).

It was different in East Anglia. There, the locals accepted glasswort as samphire and continued to pickle it. Mabey (1978) remarks that the 'old way was to pack the samphire into jars with vinegar and store them in bread ovens which were cooling down on Friday night after the baking was finished. The jars were left until Monday morning ... it seems to have been highly valued.' Even this tradition appears to have declined, and may have died out so far as the

East Anglian table is concerned. However, the revival of the fresh-fish trade supplying restaurants and commercial kitchens in the South-East, together with an appreciation of wild foods, has led to a reintroduction of samphire (mainly marsh) to fishmongers. It can be bought in many places in London.

The position of rock samphire is less secure. No one gathers it in sufficient quantity to pickle it for sale, but there are commercial kitchens which use it in their recipes in the South-West of England. Pickled samphire is still available in markets in Spain (Stobart, 1980) and in Boulogne – to name but one in France. It can also be eaten raw at the start of the season, or lightly blanched and served with melted butter. It then goes as well with lamb as with fish.

TECHNIQUE:

Marsh samphire is collected by hand from the edges of tidal creeks; it should be cut from the plant just above the base, washed, and used whilst very fresh. Sold from fish stalls, markets and wayside stalls in north Norfolk.

Rock samphire is gathered before it flowers from cliffs and rocks on the coast. After washing and blanching, it may be pickled in vinegar. Evelyn reckoned the best time to pickle it was Michaelmas (29 September); this is thought late in the year by modern cooks.

REGION OF PRODUCTION:

SOUTH ENGLAND.

Watercress

DESCRIPTION:

THE DARK GREEN LEAVES OF WATERCRESS ARE SOLD IN BUNCHES OF ABOUT 100G. FLAVOUR: PEPPERY.

HISTORY:

Watercress, *Nasturtium officinale*, picked from streams and meadows, was valued for its medicinal qualities. The herbalist John Gerard (1636) and others extolled it as an anti-scorbutic. The Italian

Castelvetro in 1614 wrote that it was 'the last green salad of the season which goes on being available all winter provided the streams are not frozen. It makes quite a pleasant salad, but since there is no alternative it always seems better that it really is. Because watercress grows in fast-running water it is very refreshing and is usually eaten raw.' There was confusion, however, between the various sorts of cress and the nasturtium flower (now called *Tropaeolum majus*). John Evelyn (1699) expresses it well: 'Cresses, Nasturtium, garden cresses; to be monthly sown: but above all the Indian [our nasturtium flower], moderately hot and aromatick, quicken the torpent spirits, and purge the brain, and are of singular effect against the scorbute [scurvy] …There is the *Nasturtium Hybernicum* commended also [the winter cress, *Barbarea verna*], and the vulgar watercress, proper in the spring, all of the same nature, tho' of different degrees, and best for raw and cold stomachs, but nourish little.'

This 'vulgar' cress did not receive much notice from cookery writers, it was perhaps beneath their notice or merely formed part of a general category of saladings. The perils of eating plants that grew in near-stagnant water fouled by animal droppings must also have militated against too general an adoption. In Flanders, there was a fondness for watercress soup, and in France 'cooks insist upon sending to table a bunch of cresses with roast fowl – even when there is salad besides' (Dallas, 1877); but neither were British customs.

The general adoption of watercress into the diet, particularly of the urban proletariat, occurred when the hygienic cultivation of watercress began in Kent in the early nineteenth century. In essence, the cress was grown in guaranteed running water. From Kent, it spread to the Thames Valley, and thence, as the expanding rail network enabled speedy transport, to the chalk streams of Hampshire and Dorset with which it is most closely connected today. The railway to these districts was even popularly dubbed 'the Watercress Line'. It was cried in the streets of London, where workmen bought it for breakfast and became as popular for sandwiches as cucumber (Mayhew, 1861).

The main areas for cultivation are the valleys of the rivers Test and Itchen, in Hampshire. Cress is also grown in Dorset and Wiltshire. A very little cultivation is still carried on in Hertfordshire and Kent. Watercress requires hard water at constant temperature; the latter is important in winter. In southern England these conditions are provided by the chalk aquifers in the counties of Hampshire, Dorset and Wiltshire; this maintains a temperature of 11°C; the beds have a gravel base and a gradual even slope to ensure the correct flow. The cress is cut by hand or harvested mechanically, cooled, washed, and packed. All watercress seed used in Britain is home-produced; in summer, beds are cleaned and replanted at frequent intervals to ensure a regular supply of young leaves, whilst in winter, crops are grown under protective covering.

REGION OF PRODUCTION:
SOUTH ENGLAND, HAMPSHIRE.

Sussex Slipcote Cheese

DESCRIPTION:
SOFT, UNPASTEURIZED SHEEP'S MILK CHEESE; AS BUTTONS OF 5CM DIAMETER, 2CM DEEP (100G), OR LOGS 18CM LONG, 6CM DEEP (1KG). COLOUR: PALE, ALMOST WHITE. FLAVOUR: LIGHT BUT CREAMY. GARLIC, AND HERB AND BLACK PEPPERCORN-FLAVOURED CHEESES ALSO MADE.

HISTORY:
Slipcote, or slipcoat, cheese has a long history in Britain. Originally, it appears to have been a full-fat cheese, and was widely known. The name may derive from the cheese breaking out of its rind as it ripened (Rance, 1982). Other British cheeses had this reputation, for instance the now-extinct Colwick. *Law's Grocer's Manual* (*c.* 1895) described slipcote as 'a rich and soft kind of cheese made of milk warm from the cow, and often with cream added. It closely resembles white butter.' It was a cheese type, rather than a regional description, though a

Victorian writer linked it especially with Yorkshire, and apparently it was known in Rutland until the First World War and, Rance says, 'remembered later as something like a Camembert, sold on straw, with a volatile coat'. Sir Kenelm Digby gave 3 recipes for slipcote from his *Closet* (1669), recalling that 'My Lady of Middlesex makes excellent slippcoat Cheese of good morning milk, putting Cream to it.' It was a soft, fresh cheese, usually wrapped in docks, nettles, grass or reeds.

Rationing discouraged the manufacture of such rich cheeses, but it is now made again, this time with sheep's rather than cow's milk.

TECHNIQUE:

Milk from local flocks is used whenever possible, preferably that from Dorset Horns. It is not pasteurized. The milk is started and vegetarian rennet added; it is left overnight. The curd is gently broken and ladled into moulds. Salt is added, as are herbs or peppercorns if required. Draining depends on season and size of cheese, but lasts 1–5 days.

REGION OF PRODUCTION:
SOUTH ENGLAND, SUSSEX.

Bedfordshire Clanger

DESCRIPTION:

AN OBLONG, BAKED PASTY MADE WITH A SUET CRUST, FILLED WITH SAVOURY AND SWEET INGREDIENTS AT OPPOSITE ENDS. DIMENSIONS: 12–14CM LONG, 6–8CM WIDE. COLOUR: GOLDEN CRUST. FLAVOUR: A SAVOURY FILLING OF MEAT, USUALLY CURED PORK, AT ONE END AND A SWEET, OFTEN APPLE, AT THE OTHER.

HISTORY:

The Bedfordshire Clanger has undergone much change in the last century. Today it is a baked pasty (with a suet crust) which has 2 fillings rather than one. Savoury meat and something sweet sit at opposite ends of a baked pie. This does not seem to have been the original form. Clangers were once a boiled suet roll, like plum duff or roly-poly. The roll contained a meat filling, and the crust was itself studded with fruit.

As a chef, it is extremely important to me to use the best-tasting, healthiest and freshest food I can find – from pork and beef to fruit and vegetables. For this reason, we at Le Manoir aux Quat'Saisons have always worked closely with our local producers, my favourite of which is Laverstoke Park. For me, farm founder Jody Scheckter and his team, through their uncompromising approach to organic farming, are already achieving excellence in their field. Jody's ambitions are extremely high – compromise doesn't exist in his approach to farming. He has surrounded himself with the best professionals in every facet of his business and he was one of the very first to understand that the quality and variety of the soil are cornerstones of successful organic farming.

The team at Laverstoke Park creates the most natural and healthy environment for their animals and crops to thrive in. They follow nature closely, carefully combining natural processes where appropriate with the latest and best scientific research, techniques and equipment. They also know that to achieve a healthy environment, plant and animal biodiversity is a vital factor, as are slower-growing traditional, older, native and rare breeds of animals.

As a result, Jody is already producing some of the best-tasting and most nutritious food available. We use Hebridean lambs from Laverstoke Park, an ancient breed of sheep originating from the islands off the west coast of Scotland. The small carcass produces the most delicious lamb, and is very tender and succulent.

Raymond Blanc

CHEF AND PROPRIETOR, LE MANOIR AUX QUAT'SAISONS, GREAT MILTON

It became a sort of complete meal in one. Compilations of English country recipes show them to have been plain, substantial food for farm labourers and other manual workers. Suet pastry enclosed a filling which varied with the affluence of the family involved (Ayrton, 1982). The poor used the only meat which was readily available, bacon; richer families used good steak or pork. Similar dishes were made in other parts of central eastern England. Poulson (1978) mentions a bacon clanger, filled with bacon, sage and onion, from the Thames valley; a similar dish was known in Leicestershire as a Quorn bacon roll.

No-one has offered a derivation of clanger. Wright (1896–1905) cites 'clang' as a Northamptonshire dialect word meaning 'to eat voraciously'. The Bedfordshire Clanger may have developed in response to local employment patterns (Mabey, 1978). Many women were employed in the straw-hat industry and the clanger, boiling slowly for hours unattended, was a complete hot meal for those arriving home from work. Clangers are now made because there is a local taste for them. There are even clanger-eating contests at local fairs and festivities. Clangers have now evolved into a baked dish. This reflects the evolution of British cooking methods away from long boiling to dry baking, more convenient once domestic gas or electric cookers were universally available. Old recipes sometimes called for the boiled rolls to be dried in a low oven before consumption.

TECHNIQUE:

Bedfordshire Clangers made for sale are less elaborate than those produced at home. The fillings are prepared first; meat is cut into small dice, onions chopped, apples peeled and sliced. An English suet crust is made: plain flour and chopped suet (2:1), salt and enough water for a coherent dough. The pastry is rolled out and cut to oblongs twice the size of the finished clanger. Small mounds of the savoury and sweet fillings are placed in opposing ends divided by a strip of pastry. The pastry is folded over to enclose the fillings. The edges and the area around the central dividing strip are sealed, and the surface glazed with egg. It is baked at 210°C for 30 minutes.

Berkshire Pig

DESCRIPTION:

DRESSED CARCASS WEIGHT 36–45KG. BERKSHIRE PIGS HAVE A SHORT, DEEP BODY, ALTHOUGH THE DEVELOPMENT OF LONGER ANIMALS HAS BEEN RECENTLY ENCOURAGED. ALTHOUGH THE BREED HAS A BLACK SKIN, THIS BECOMES WHITE IF THE CARCASS IS CORRECTLY PREPARED. WHEN REARED EXTENSIVELY, THE MEAT IS DEEPER PINK THAN NORMAL; IT IS FINELY TEXTURED WITH A SWEET FLAVOUR AND A HIGH PROPORTION OF LEAN TO FAT.

HISTORY:

This breed was developed in the Thames valley in the late 1700s. Early specimens are described as large-boned and tawny, red or white spotted with black. Not many years later, it was made more compact, more lightly boned and faster-maturing by interbreeding with Chinese or east Asian stock. The improved Berkshire was entirely black or white.

Mrs Beeton (1861) listed Berkshires among native British stock and praises it for a fine, delicate skin and a great aptitude to fatten. The British Berkshire Society was founded in the 1880s but the fortunes of the race declined in this century when it proved too slow-maturing and fat in comparison with modern bloodlines. Since the 1970s, there has been renewed interest and numbers are slowly recovering.

TECHNIQUE:

The majority of Berkshires are kept outdoors, grubbing for food on grassland. They are hardy, can withstand cold weather and do not suffer sunburn. Although they can feed themselves adequately by foraging, most breeders supplement with barley or oats as well as vitamins. It is especially important that carcasses of Berkshires are carefully scalded as the black hairs and pigment of the skin, considered unsightly when the meat is presented for sale, can be entirely removed by correct treatment. This is important for the British market as pork is almost always roasted with the skin intact. Berkshire is noted as pork with excellent crackling: an English sine qua non.

REGION OF PRODUCTION:
SOUTH ENGLAND.

Chitterlings

DESCRIPTION:
CHITTERLINGS ARE COOKED PIGS' INTESTINES; THERE ARE SEVERAL METHODS OF PRESENTING THESE FOR SALE. THEY MAY BE MADE INTO PLAITS; OR CUT IN 6–8CM LENGTHS, AND SOLD BY WEIGHT; OR MADE INTO SLABS, THE PIECES HELD TOGETHER IN JELLY. THE 2 LATTER OFTEN INCLUDE PIECES OF PIGS' MAW (STOMACH) CUT INTO STRIPS AND MIXED WITH THE CHITTERLINGS. COLOUR: VARIABLE, OFF-WHITE THROUGH PALE GREY-PINK TO DEEP PINK; THE JELLIED SLABS ARE CUT INTO SLICES AT RIGHT ANGLES TO THE LENGTH OF THE CHITTERLINGS, GIVING AN ATTRACTIVE MARBLED APPEARANCE. FLAVOUR: BRINED, JELLIED CHITTERLING TASTES SIMILAR TO LEAN BACON.

HISTORY:
The word chitterling is of uncertain derivation but has been used in English since at least the thirteenth century for the small intestines of animals, especially pigs, when used for food. At one time it seems to have also referred to a type of sausage made from them (akin to a French *andouillette*), but latterly has come to mean simply the intestines, cleaned and prepared.

Their preparation is not elaborate. Since the late twentieth century they are a minority taste, seen as a poverty food and regarded as old-fashioned. It is recognized that they are more popular in some regions than others. Their stronghold is the South and South-West, where pigs have long been reared in huge numbers.

Chitterlings are sold cooked and can be eaten cold with vinegar or mustard; or they can be heated by frying with bacon, or by boiling.

TECHNIQUE:

Pigs' small intestines are prepared by turning them inside out and cleaning; they are cut into short lengths or plaited. The chitterlings may be soaked in brine overnight if desired. They are cooked in boiling salted water for about 30 minutes. As they give off a pungent smell in the cooking, some butchers now prefer to enclose them in vacuum bags before putting them into the water. After this they are ready for sale. Some manufacturers pressed chitterlings and maw in a mould to cool, the liquor forming a jelly around them. This is sliced and vacuum-packed for sale.

REGION OF PRODUCTION:

SOUTH ENGLAND; SOUTH WEST ENGLAND.

Oxford Sausage

DESCRIPTION:

A FRESH PORK AND VEAL SAUSAGE; 6–8 SAUSAGES TO THE LB (450G). FORM: FAIRLY SHORT AND PLUMP. COLOUR: SLIGHTLY PALER PINK THAN THE AVERAGE, WITH PROMINENT HERB FLECKS. FLAVOUR: A GOOD BALANCE OF LEMON AND HERBS.

HISTORY:

In 1779, the Reverend Dr Warner wrote to his friend George Selwyn, 'I shall also order some New College puddings and Oxford sausages, and hope to bring you a hare.' (Jesse, 1901) These sausages were already famous. In 1726, John Nott gave a recipe for 'Sausages called Oxford Skates' which closely resembles recipes still known. It is a mixture of pork, veal and beef suet, quite highly seasoned. White (1932) has printed similar recipes from the following 200 years. In all of them, the mixture was rolled into cylinders or patties, floured and fried. If Oxford sausages were skinless, it goes without saying that Cambridge sausages (also celebrated in the past) were stuffed into skins.

Mrs Rundell (1807) mentions the addition of a little soaked bread in her instructions, suggesting the recipe had then begun to evolve along lines similar to other British sausages. Dallas (1877) noted that the mixture was pressed 'down close in a pan for use. It may be stuffed in skins like other sausage meat; but is generally rolled out as wanted, and either fried in fresh butter of a brown colour or broiled over a clear fire.' Oxford sausages were less remarked in the twentieth century but were still known, and Florence White records correspondence about them, including the fact they could still be bought in Oxford market in the early 1930s and that a similar skinless sausage was found in Cornwall. Finney's guide for pork butchers (1915) included an Oxford seasoning which included sage and coriander; he also had recipes for Oxford beef sausages.

In recent years British fresh sausages generally have suffered from the application of mass-production techniques. Recently, more interest has been taken in the subject, and new companies are researching and using recipes based on those from the eighteenth century.

TECHNIQUE:

There are 2 differences between Oxford sausages of the past and those known today. The first is in the composition: beef suet is rarely used now, as it produces a sausage which is dense and heavy to modern taste. Secondly, the sausages are now put into casings. A manufacturer who has recently begun to make Oxford sausages based on old recipes uses shoulder pork from locally produced, extensively farmed pigs. Equal quantities of veal, plus a small amount of cereal form the basis; the meat is minced with a little rusk, and seasoned with herbs, salt, lemon zest and spices, and then filled into narrow hog casings and hand-linked.

REGION OF PRODUCTION:

SOUTH ENGLAND, OXFORD.

Cottage Loaf

DESCRIPTION:

A CIRCULAR LOAF WITH A LARGE TOPKNOT (USUALLY ONE-THIRD THE
SIZE OF THE MAIN PART); THE SURFACE IS SOMETIMES SLASHED TO GIVE
A ROSETTE EFFECT WHEN RISING IS COMPLETED. A SMALL LOAF IS
ABOUT 100MM HIGH, 180–200MM DIAMETER. WEIGHT: 400G (SMALL),
800G (LARGE). COLOUR: DEEP GOLD CRUST WITH PALER, LESS BAKED
AREAS IN THE NOTCHES. FLAVOUR: THE SHAPE OF THE LOAF GIVES A
HIGHER RATIO OF CRUST TO CRUMB THAN OBTAINED WITH TIN LOAVES.

HISTORY:

The earliest reference to the distinctive shape known as a 'cottage loaf'
cited by the *Oxford English Dictionary* comes from the 1840s. How
long they were made before then is not obvious, although a description
by Edlin (1805) makes it clear that loaves of the cottage type were
being made. Until the Second World War, they were perhaps the most
common shape available in England. In Scotland, they were only
occasionally made but when they were, they were flatter and lighter. By
contrast, Welsh loaves and those from the Midlands had a closer,
cakier texture.

The moulding of a cottage loaf is not easy. Inadequate
craftsmanship could make the halves separate or cause alarming tilts
and eccentricities. Perhaps this is why Kirkland (1907) noticed that
London cottage loaves had smaller topknots.

No complete explanation of the development of the shape is likely. A
parallel may be drawn with the shape of *pain chapeau*, found in the
Finistère district of Brittany. The cob loaf was the simplest, round, oven-
bottom bread in the English baker's repertoire. Oven-bottom breads
were crustier and more flavourful than loaves cooked in tins (as were
most often produced in Scotland, for example, and which became
almost universal with the industrialization of British breadmaking). The
word cob meant nothing more than a small lump. A similar loaf shape
was the coburg, a London form named in honour of the marriage of
Queen Victoria to Prince Albert of Saxe-Coburg. This was a cob loaf

with extra slashes across the top. The cottage loaf could be likened to 2 cobs piled on top of each other. As it became necessary to increase the output of bakeries in the face of growing demand as England industrialized and urbanized, so a cottage loaf would greatly increase the production of each oven load. It is also possible that the shape was fostered by the availability of fine, high-protein white flour with the advent of roller milling and imports of hard wheat from North America.

TECHNIQUE:

No particular dough is reserved to this shape, but it is best if it is stiff in texture. After mixing and bulk fermentation, the dough is scaled off into pieces for the tops and bottoms (top and bottom loaves was a Chichester (Sussex) name for this shape). The top is joined to the bottom by pressing through the centre of the top with the fingers. After a final proof and, if required, slashing the top surface, the loaf is baked on the oven bottom at 230°C for 60 minutes.

REGION OF PRODUCTION:
SOUTH ENGLAND.

Isle of Wight Doughnut

DESCRIPTION:

ROUGHLY SPHERICAL FRIED DOUGH, 70MM DIAMETER. WEIGHT: ABOUT 75G. COLOUR: GOLDEN BROWN OUTSIDE, DUSTED WITH SUGAR; PALE GOLD INSIDE, WITH SULTANAS AND A JAM FILLING. FLAVOUR: SWEETISH, SHORT-TEXTURED.

HISTORY:

Deep-fried pastry and fritters are not well represented in British food traditions. An exception seems to be the Isle of Wight, on the English south coast. Here, there are several variations on the theme including doughnuts filled with currants and tied in the shape of a knot and an apple-filled one in a turnover (half circle) shape. In the mid-nineteenth century a yeast-raised doughnut with a filling of raisins and candied peel was made there; a recipe was given by Eliza Acton (1845). She noted that at certain times they were made in large quantities and were drained of their fat on very clean straw. The dough was flavoured with allspice, cinnamon, cloves and mace. Another recipe was collected by the local Women's Institute in the 1930s. It is similar, apart from a reduction in spices to nutmeg alone. Oral tradition states that until about 30 years ago, a few shops displayed these doughnuts piled up in their windows and sold nothing else. The doughnuts made at present are produced to a recipe belonging to a long-established bakery in Newport.

TECHNIQUE:

Published recipes call for plain flour, butter and sugar in the proportions 6:1:1. The butter is rubbed into the flour, followed by the sugar and grated nutmeg; this is made into a soft yeasted dough with milk and egg. After fermentation, pieces about the size of tangerines are nipped off. A hollow is made which is filled with a few raisins and a piece of candied peel and, in some recipes, lemon zest. The dough is wrapped around and smoothed over to make a ball. They were cooked in lard – now more often vegetable oil – at 160–170°C. They are turned once during cooking, when golden brown. Then they are drained and dusted with icing sugar.

REGION OF PRODUCTION:

SOUTH ENGLAND, ISLE OF WIGHT.

Cider Cake

DESCRIPTION:

A CIRCULAR CAKE (OCCASIONALLY SQUARE), 140–200MM DIAMETER, 30–40MM DEEP. WEIGHT: 450–700G. COLOUR: PALE GOLDEN EXTERIOR, DEEP CREAM CRUMB. FLAVOUR: RICH, WITH AFTERTASTE OF CIDER; SOMETIMES SPICED AND WITH DRIED FRUIT.

HISTORY:

Elizabeth Ayrton (1980) remarks that cider cake is often met in Oxfordshire, Herefordshire, Worcestershire and Gloucestershire, that several recipes from the 1800s are known and that they all use bicarbonate of soda as a raising agent. In this form, the cake cannot date much before the 1850s, when baking soda was first used as a leaven. The technique for mixing the cake is also relatively modern. There is a possible connection between cider cakes and vinegar cakes. These last rely on bicarbonate of soda neutralized by the acetic acid in vinegar to make them rise; English cider, which is very dry and rather acid, makes a good alternative. Cider cakes are made in all cider-producing counties, and are sometimes called after the relevant county. Examples are recorded from Suffolk, Somerset, Dorset, Gloucester, Hereford and Worcester, and Oxford.

TECHNIQUE:

Flour, butter and sugar are used in the proportions 2:1:1. Some add spices; nutmeg is the most common. There are 2 methods of mixing. The first sees the fat rubbed into the flour, the sugar stirred through, and eggs, cider, dried fruit and nuts added as required. The second is more elaborate: the butter and sugar are beaten together until fluffy, mixed with eggs and beaten again. Then half the flour, combined with spice and bicarbonate of soda, is beaten in. The cider is added, and the mixture stirred until it begins to froth. The remaining flour is immediately stirred through. The cake is baked at 200°C for 40–50 minutes.

REGION OF PRODUCTION:

SOUTH ENGLAND.

Lardy Cake

DESCRIPTION:

RECTANGULAR OR ROUND CAKES; ONE FROM OXFORD WAS 180MM LONG, 110MM WIDE, 30MM DEEP; ONE FROM GLOUCESTER WAS A LOOSE SPIRAL 160MM DIAMETER, 40MM DEEP. WEIGHT: THE OXFORD EXAMPLE WAS 500G, THE GLOUCESTER 250G. COLOUR: DEEP GOLD, STICKY AND SHINY UNDERNEATH, SPECKLED WITH DRIED FRUIT, PALE, ALMOST WHITE CRUMB; THE CAKE RANGES FROM LAYERED AND FLAKY PUFF PASTRY TO A SIMPLE, ROLLED SHEET OF DOUGH. FLAVOUR AND TEXTURE: SWEET WITH A FLAKY APPEARANCE WHEN CUT; SOLID, CHEWY.

This cake is based on lard, the fat most commonly used in pig-rearing regions of Britain, which is incorporated into dough taken from the main batch at bread making. Wright (1896–1905) associates it with Oxfordshire, Berkshire and Wiltshire but it was more widely known than that. Most counties appear to have made a version at one time, and they varied a little according to the fat used. Some called for the 'flead' or 'flare' – the kidney fat – to be used raw. Others used scratchings, the residue after fat has been rendered. Mayhew (1861) records trays of flare cakes for sale on the streets of London. As a food of the poor and of country people, lardy cakes escaped the attention of many early recipe collectors. They are now principally identified with the South, especially north and west of London. There are differences, especially in shape, between counties, but not of basic principle. Variant names include shaley or sharley cake (Wiltshire); dripping cake or 'drips' (Gloucestershire); bread cake (Shropshire). Apples or spices such as cinnamon may be included for variety.

TECHNIQUE:

Home cooks tend to make richer cakes than commercial bakers. Ingredients are dough, sugar, lard and mixed fruit and peel in the ratio of 3 or 4:1:1:1. The dough is taken from the main batch after bulk fermentation and rolled into a rectangle; two thirds of this is spread with one third of the lard, and scattered with one third of the fruit and peel and one third of the sugar; the dough is folded and turned, and the process repeated twice. The final turn is arranged so the dough is shaped into a roll. The cake may then be scored for later cutting. It is proved for 1 hour and baked for 45 minutes at 220°C. It is turned upside down to cool to prevent it sticking; this is said to encourage the lard to run back through the cake.

REGION OF PRODUCTION:

SOUTH ENGLAND, WILTSHIRE.

Barley Wine: Thomas Hardy's Ale

DESCRIPTION:

COLOUR VARIES ACCORDING TO AGE BUT IS OFTEN A DEEP COPPERY BROWN WITH A HEAVY AND MALTY FLAVOUR. THOMAS HARDY'S ALE IS SWEET, HEAVY BODIED, WITH FRUIT AND CHOCOLATE OVERTONES. IT IS 12 PER CENT ALCOHOL BY VOLUME, STRONGER THAN ANY NORMAL BEER AND MANY WINES.

HISTORY:

Earliest references to barley wine by name date from the twentieth century (*OED*). Jackson (1993) considers, 'the romantic term "barley wine" may have been coined by rural home-brewers to describe their most impressively potent efforts'. There is no evidence that the name came from the use of wine yeasts. It is now often employed by brewers to describe their strongest ale, but the style is older than the name. It is kin to the dark beers known earlier as porter. The archaic northern dialect word 'stingo' has also been used. In Scotland, such powerful beers are known as 'wee heavy'.

Dorchester developed as a centre of the brewing industry during the eighteenth century, due partly to a chalk aquifer in the strata below the town. Richard Bradley (1736) wrote of its fine beer with 'a strength of malt and hops in it' to last 4 years. '[It] is esteem'd prefereable to most of the Malt-Liquor in England,' he continued, '[for] it is for the most part brew'd of chalky water.'

Hardy himself wrote a lyrical description of Dorchester ale in *The Trumpet Major* (1880). The drink which now bears his name, however, is recent: developed in 1968 to honour the then prime minister, Harold Macmillan, whose family was Hardy's publisher. Breweries who produce barley wines often give them names of characters, fictional or real. Eldridge Pope, the brewers of this beer, were founded in 1837.

TECHNIQUE:

A lightly kilned ale malt is used for Thomas Hardy's Ale. The wort is hopped with English varieties, and a top-fermenting yeast is used for a primary fermentation which lasts for approximately 10 days. After

When I got my first job on a newspaper it was as cookery writer for the *Daily Mail*, and I was lucky not to lose it in the first month. I had written a recipe for Oxford Marmalade – you know the one: made with bitter Seville oranges, chunky and dark with treacle – but I had written it by hand and forgotten to cross the 't' in treacle. This meant that '2 tbs' was printed as '2 lbs'. Since the rest of the ingredients only amounted to ten oranges and a kilo of sugar, this had disaster potential. And a disaster it was.

You would not believe the number of people who just accept what they read in newspapers. The *Daily Mail* switchboard went white-hot with complaints about the black caramel in readers' saucepans. We had to reimburse readers for a lot of ingredient costs and quite a few saucepans which were damaged beyond repair. So when a woman rang up and suggested we let her know how much extra sugar and how many extra oranges she should add to the mixture to get the proportions right again, I thought, 'Good, this is how we rescue the situation – we just get everyone to make extra marmalade for next year, plus a few pots for the village fête and so on.' Until, that is, we worked out that each reader would need to make about eighty jars of marmalade. We reimbursed her like everyone else.

The day after publication I found what looked like a letter bomb on my desk. Well, I knew I'd got the recipe wrong, but I thought bombing was going a bit far. I could tell it was a bomb because, this being the time of the IRA letter bomb campaign, we'd all had bomb training. If you got a suspicious package, especially one like this, which had something squashy in the middle and what felt like wires sticking out each side, you called the security desk and they sent a copper in a flak jacket who took it away.

Eventually the copper brought it back. It contained a piece of marmalade toffee with a dental brace, complete with two teeth embedded in it. And a very large orthodontist's bill.

Prue Leith

COOKERY EDITOR, FOOD COLUMNIST AND BROADCASTER, AND FOUNDER OF LEITH'S RESTAURANT this, the beer is re-yeasted for a secondary fermentation and warm-conditioned for 3–6 months, after which the beer is drawn off the sediment and given a further conditioning in cold store for 1–3 months. Yeast is added several times during this time, as the high sugar and alcohol content affect it significantly. When considered ready to leave the brewery, the beer is re-yeasted again and bottled for distribution. It will improve up to its best in the bottle at 5–7 years and will keep for 25 years.

REGION OF PRODUCTION:
SOUTH ENGLAND, DORSET.

Elderflower Cordial

DESCRIPTION:
A PALE STRAW COLOUR AND TRANSPARENT. IT HAS A STRONG AROMA OF ELDERFLOWER AND MUSCAT AND IS BOTH SWEET AND SHARP TO THE TASTE.

HISTORY:
Most British soft drinks are fruit based; this is singular in being made from flowers. Rather aptly, the elder was once considered of value for treating the heart and circulation.

TECHNIQUE:
Elderflowers, gathered when fully open (late May to late June), are steeped with sugar, lemon and citric acid for 5 days, before the cordial is strained and bottled. Commercial producers use methods which are a scaled-up version of this. There are differences in the treatment of the flowers after picking: one producer mills and presses them to produce a juice which is used to flavour the essence; another stores them in a solution of sugar and citric acid. Dried flowers are also used in some cordials.

REGION OF PRODUCTION:
SOUTH ENGLAND AND NATIONWIDE.

Single-Variety Apple Juice

DESCRIPTION:

FRESH PRESSED APPLE JUICE IS OFTEN PALE YELLOW-GREEN AND
CLOUDY. SOME IS FILTERED. THE FLAVOUR DEPENDS ON THE VARIETY
OF APPLE. MANY HAVE COMPLEX FLORAL, FRUITY, SPICY AND NUTTY
OVERTONES. PRODUCTION FROM INDIGENOUS VARIETIES IS AS
PARTICULAR TO BRITAIN AS THE APPLES THEMSELVES.

HISTORY:

Apples have been pressed for juice, primarily as the first step in cider-making, for centuries. Commercial juice production in England began in the 1930s and by the 1970s had become a large industry. At this time, most so-called juice was made from concentrate mixed with water. The development of single-variety juices has arisen from a growing interest in the different flavours of apples and from a need to diversify into new markets for agricultural produce. Cox's Orange Pippin and Bramley's Seedling, favourite long-keeping English apples, are much used (and often blended together when a single-variety juice is not required); other varieties are pressed when available.

TECHNIQUE:

All producers begin with milling and pressing the apples as if for cider. The juice may then be left to clear and be filtered before pasteurizing. Both flash-pasteurizing at a high temperature and a lower-temperature, longer method are used. Some add vitamin C as an antioxidant.

REGION OF PRODUCTION:

SOUTH ENGLAND.

South East England

Blenheim Orange Apple

DESCRIPTION:

A LATE-SEASON APPLE SUITABLE FOR DESSERT AND COOKING. DESCRIBED BY MORGAN & RICHARDS (1993) AS MEDIUM-LARGE (5–8CM DIAMETER); FLAT-ROUND, WITH ROUNDED RIBS, SLIGHTLY CROWNED; HAVING A BROAD DEEP BASIN, WITH A LITTLE RUSSET; THE EYE LARGE AND OPEN, THE SEPALS SEPARATED AT THE BASE; THE CAVITY OF MEDIUM WIDTH AND DEPTH, RUSSET LINED; THE STALK SHORT AND THICK; THE COLOUR IS CHARACTERIZED BY AN ORANGE-RED FLUSH WITH A FEW RED STRIPES OVER GREENISH YELLOW OR GOLD, WITH RUSSET PATCHES AND VEINS; THE FLESH IS PALE CREAM AND SLIGHTLY CRUMBLY; THE FLAVOUR IS DESCRIBED AS ADDICTIVE, PLAIN, FLAVOURED WITH NUTS, QUITE SWEET.

HISTORY:

This apple was discovered in the mid-eighteenth century growing against a boundary wall of Blenheim Park, the seat of the dukes of Marlborough in Oxfordshire. A local workman moved it into his garden and the tree became famous for the colour and quantity of fruit. Initially it was known as Kempster's Pippin but was renamed in the early nineteenth century with the consent of the Duke of the time. It was then widely grown and considered one of the finest of English apple types. It declined in importance when production for market became more methodical as it is biennial in habit. Interest in old varieties has led to new attention being paid to this and other less well-known apples.

Early in its season, in late September, Blenheim Orange is often chosen for cooking: it keeps its shape well and is used for dishes where appearance is important or a firm purée necessary. Later, during the following month, it has developed in flavour sufficiently to be offered as a dessert apple, thought also excellent with cheese.

TECHNIQUE:

Optimum pollination time for this variety is mid-May. The tree is vigorous. Blenheim Orange is described by experts as easy to grow but difficult to crop, as it is biennial in habit, cropping heavily every other year. Fruit buds are produced partly at the tips of new growth. The variety is resistant to mildew. Picking is by hand in late September and early October. Little organized storage of this apple takes place because it is not widely grown on a commercial scale; it used to be stored for use as a dessert apple in late autumn.

REGION OF PRODUCTION:
KENT.

Grenadier Apple

DESCRIPTION:

EARLY-SEASON COOKING APPLE. DESCRIBED BY MORGAN & RICHARDS (1993) AS LARGE (DIAMETER 7.5–8CM); THE SHAPE IS ROUND-CONICAL, QUITE IRREGULAR, FIBBED AND FLAT SIDED, WITH A NARROW, QUITE SHALLOW BASIN THAT IS RIBBED AND PUCKERED; THE EYE SMALL AND CLOSED, THE CORE OPEN, THE CAVITY BROAD AND QUITE DEEP AND THE STALK SHORT AND THICK; THE SKIN IS GREEN-YELLOW WITH SCARF SKIN AT BASE, AND THE FLESH WHITE; IT IS SHARP-FLAVOURED.

HISTORY:

The British apple market is distinctive in having several varieties that are grown specifically for cooking. These disintegrate into a purée more readily than eating apples (having more malic acid). Other countries tend to grow varieties (and develop sympathetic recipes) that are used for both cooking and eating.

The Grenadier is the first cooking apple to reach the market at the start of the English apple season in late summer. Its origin is unknown; it was exhibited in the 1860s by one Charles Turner, a nurseryman in Slough (Buckinghamshire), and was commercialized in the 1880s. It cooks to a purée. Another early-season cooking apple, of the type known as codlin (a sour apple which cooks to a froth), which came to prominence just before the First World War was the Emneth Early, raised at Emneth in Cambridgeshire. It was important for many years, but is now rarely seen for sale.

Grenadier is good for dishes in which a frothy purée is needed. A drink made with codlin apples is 'lambswool', in which the cooked pulp is floated on top of hot spiced ale.

TECHNIQUE:
Optimum pollination time for Grenadier is early to mid-May; the tree is of medium vigour and is a heavy cropper. Picking is by hand in mid-August. Grading is by diameter (sizes are set according to variety) and by quality (EU standards, for appearance) into Grade 1 or Grade 2. Grenadier can be stored for only about 2 months.

REGION OF PRODUCTION:
SOUTH EAST ENGLAND, KENT.

Kentish Cobnut

DESCRIPTION:
FRESH HAZELNUTS. AT THE START OF THE SEASON, COBNUTS HAVE GREEN HUSKS AND SHELLS, AND PALE MILKY KERNELS; AS IT PROGRESSES, THE SHELLS TURN BROWN AND THE FLAVOUR OF THE KERNELS BECOMES MORE INTENSE. THE KENTISH COB PRODUCES A MEDIUM-LARGE NUT, THIN-SHELLED AND ELONGATED WITH A LONG HUSK, GROWING IN CLUSTERS OF 2–5 FRUITS. THE DIFFERENCES BETWEEN CULTIVARS ARE SHAPE AND SIZE. FLAVOUR: MILKY, SLIGHTLY SWEET, CRUNCHY TEXTURE.

The hazelnut, *Corylus avallana*, is indigenous to all of Britain and there is evidence of its use for food from archaeological sites from the Neolithic onwards. Hazelnuts have been cultivated since at least the sixteenth century but these seem mainly to have been another species, native to south-eastern Europe, *Corylus maxima*, which is distinguished by the length of its husk. The name filbert seems always to have referred to nuts with long husks which covered the nut itself. Cobnut was used to describe 'our hedge Nut or Hasell Nut Tree', while filberts were 'that which groweth in gardens and orchards' (Gerard, 1597).

Kent was already famous for its Filberts when John Evelyn wrote his great treatise on forestry, Sylva, in 1664. They continued to be grown as part of a mixed husbandry with hops, apples and cherries (Roach, 1985). There were 3 or 4 important varieties: the one known as the 'Kentish' Filbert was the white-skinned.

This was ultimately displaced, either from 1812 or from 1830 (depending which Lambert was in fact responsible for its introduction), by an improved breed called Lambert's Filbert. It was inconvenient that history never guaranteed the identity of its progenitor. Lovers of simplicity will also decry the renaming of Lambert's Filbert as the Kentish Cobnut, but that is what happened around the turn of the century.

Mrs Beeton (1861) wrote, 'It is supposed that, within a few miles of Maidstone, in Kent, there are more Filberts grown than in all England besides; and it is from that place that the London market is supplied.' By the early 1900s, over 7,000 acres (approximately 1,750 hectares), mostly in Kent, was given over to hazelnuts, and substantial quantities were exported to the USA. There had been much experiment with different varieties, although the Kentish Cob reigned supreme. Thereafter, nut production declined greatly, until only a few specialist growers remained. The reasons are largely to do with changes in agricultural and orcharding practice in Kent, as well as the high level of handiwork involved in maintaining the cropping trees. Little research has been undertaken to improve strains. Kent remains the chief centre of production, but there are orchards in Sussex, Devon and Worcestershire.

TECHNIQUE:

Two or three varieties of hazelnut are often grown together to ensure pollination. They require a sheltered, well-drained site. In modern practice, they are grown as bush trees on stems 35–40cm high, and planted in rows 5 metres apart. Older 'plats' (the local term for a hazelnut orchard) may be planted more closely. Close planted trees are pruned by hand; mechanical pruning can be carried out in more widely spaced, modern plats. The trees are routinely treated with fungicide, although experiments are being carried out in the organic production of hazelnuts. Picking is by hand. Some plats are marketed as pick-your-own. A hectare of trees produces about 4 tonnes of nuts per annum.

REGION OF PRODUCTION:
SOUTH EAST ENGLAND.

Leveller Gooseberry

DESCRIPTION:

A DESSERT FRUIT THAT IS LARGE, YELLOW AND SWEET.

HISTORY:

The gooseberry is usually a fruit more suitable for cooking, needing considerable sweetening for palatability unless used as a savoury accompaniment to meat or fish. But Leveller is a variety raised by J. Greenhalgh in Ashton-under-Lyne (Lancashire) in 1851 that became an important dessert fruit. Roach (1995) remarks that it was, and still is, grown in the Chailey-Newick district of Sussex, 'where the cultivation of large-sized Leveller berries for the dessert trade has reached a very high degree of perfection.' The berries have been grown in this area for the London market since before World War II.

The area in East Sussex associated with the growing of this variety for the dessert market is sandy and highly suitable, producing a berry which ripens well with a very sweet flavour. The fruit is gathered by hand in late July or early August; it must be picked when it is just ripe and marketed straight away.

Those who grow gooseberries for show prune the bushes severely and strip most of the fruit early in the season, leaving only a few berries to attain the largest possible size.

REGION OF PRODUCTION:
SOUTH EAST ENGLAND, EAST SUSSEX.

Medlar

DESCRIPTION:
MEDLARS ARE SMALL FRUIT (3–4CM DIAMETER), WEIGHING ABOUT 15G. THEY LOOK LIKE BROWN-SKINNED APPLES, BUT HAVE A CUP-SHAPED DEPRESSION, KNOWN AS THE EYE, BETWEEN THE CALYX LOBES. COLOUR: GREEN-PURPLE WITH A SLIGHT GLOSS WHEN FRESH; PURPLE-BROWN, DULL AND SOFT WHEN BLETTED. FLAVOUR: SWEET-ACID.

HISTORY:
The medlar, *Mespilus germanica*, is a native of Transcaucasia and made its long journey into northern Europe after its adoption by Greece and Rome. It may even have been brought to Britain by the Romans – a single seed has been excavated at Silchester – and it was certainly cultivated here during the Middle Ages. The hedge-row specimens that are still found, especially in the South-East, are probably escapees from this early cultivation (Roach, 1985).

When English garden varieties were first described and codified, there were not many sorts of medlar held in high esteem – the most celebrated were the Dutch and the Neapolitan. Thus, by and large, it remained until the end of the eighteenth century when a new variety, or so it seemed, was named: the Nottingham. This appears in fact to be a Neapolitan, but muddled or renamed. The re-baptism stuck, and Nottingham it is to this day. There were some new cultivars developed in the Victorian years, but what perhaps makes the medlar quintessentially British was the enjoyment of the bletted (rotten) fruit by drinkers of port at the end of a meal. Not everyone appreciated these 'wineskins of brown morbidity' (D.H. Lawrence, quoted by Davidson, 1991) and their number reduced as time went on, but their use as a jelly which accompanies meats has seen their survival in a sphere wider than the private gardens of a handful of connoisseurs.

TECHNIQUE:

Medlars are propagated by grafting or budding. Various species have been used to provide rootstock; today, the quince is most commonly employed. The fruit are left on the trees until late autumn and may be quite hard when hand-picked. At this stage they are considered astringent and inedible. The fruit is stored in moist bran or sawdust until it becomes brown and soft. Effectively, this is a controlled rotting of the fruit. They used to be brought to the table in a dish still covered with bran or sawdust and cleaned off by the diners who scraped out the pulp to eat with sugar and cream, and to accompany port.

REGION OF PRODUCTION:
SOUTH EAST ENGLAND.

Strawberry (Royal Sovereign)

DESCRIPTION:

ROYAL SOVEREIGN HAS SMALL TO MEDIUM ROUNDED BERRIES OF A BRIGHT INTENSE RED, AND IS STILL THOUGHT BY MANY TO HAVE THE BEST FLAVOUR OF ALL BRITISH VARIETIES. MODERN STRAWBERRY VARIETIES TEND TO HAVE MUCH BIGGER, POINTED FRUIT AND A LESS INTENSE FLAVOUR.

HISTORY:

Although wood strawberries, *Fragaria vesca*, are native to Britain, the history of the strawberry in its modern form really begins in the early

nineteenth century. At this time, Michael Keen, a market gardener in Isleworth (Middlesex), used the Chilean strawberry (*F. chiloensis*) to produce improved varieties. The first of these was Keen's Imperial; the second which he raised, Keen's Seedling, caused a sensation, and became very important both in its own right and as a parent of other varieties. There was much interest in strawberry growing during the mid-nineteenth century. One of the most influential of Victorian nurserymen, Thomas Laxton at Bedford, bred Royal Sovereign. This was esteemed for its appearance and flavour and for the fact that it cropped early.

Royal Sovereign lost commercial favour around the time of World War II as producers, driven by necessity to cultivate disease-resistant stock and by the changing needs of processors, began using the Cambridge varieties (bred from the 1930s at the Horticultural Research Station of Cambridge University) and their descendants. For many years, Royal Sovereign was grown only by amateurs, but interest is reviving among commercial producers on the south-east coast of England. This region came into its own as a centre of market gardening at the end of the Victorian period. London, its chief customer, had outgrown its eighteenth-century envelope and was fast expanding into land on its western side which had until then been the main area of commercial gardening. Simultaneously, efficient railway transport enabled producers to base themselves further away than those who had depended on waterborne delivery, carriage on foot or by cart, or conveyance in panniers slung each side of a donkey. The counties along the south-eastern coast of England have been noted areas for strawberry production for over 100 years. Hampshire was known for its early strawberries, a trade now severely eroded by foreign imports.

TECHNIQUE:

Strawberries are now grown from virus-free runners produced by specialist growers. The old method was to grow under glass cloches, now superseded by polythene tunnels. Soil sterilization is also practised to control disease. In the old days, the ground was mulched with straw. The berries are grown both for dessert and processing. Royal Sovereign is a dessert variety which is grown by similar methods to other strawberries, but requires special care in handling as the berries are delicate and soft. Cambridge Favourite is regarded as a good dual-purpose type. The growth of pick-your-own farms has meant that many people have access to supplies of very fresh strawberries.

REGION OF PRODUCTION:
SOUTH EAST ENGLAND.

Victoria Plum

DESCRIPTION:

A VICTORIA PLUM WEIGHS 30–50G AND HAS DARK RED SKIN, PALE GREEN FLESH, AND A GOOD SWEET-ACID BALANCE OF FLAVOUR.

HISTORY:

The cultivated plum has been known in Britain since Roman times. Plums continued to be grown in Britain through the medieval period, with new varieties being introduced in the fifteenth century (Roach, 1985). The eighteenth-century varieties, including Fotheringham, Coe's Golden Drop (much used as a parent for good quality, late-season dessert plums), Magnum Bonum, Damascenes, and Gage were delicious and valuable, but it is the work of the Victorian nurserymen that has had most lasting significance. They raised several varieties still grown today, including Early Rivers and Czar. Several local varieties, including Aylesbury Prune, were also widely grown for drying. One of the few local seedlings which has become important in recent years is Marjories, which was discovered growing in Berkshire in 1912.

However, the Victoria plum is the most popular in modern Britain. It was a chance seedling from Alderton in Sussex found in 1840. Development took place in a nursery at Brixton, south London. It soon became established as a commercial variety in the main orcharding areas of southern England. It was used for crossing in experiments to produce new breeds in the early 1900s, especially by the Laxton brothers; although several were introduced, they have failed to maintain a place in commercial production.

Victorias now provide the majority of dessert plums, most of those for commerce grown in Kent. It is also the most ubiquitous breed in English gardens: it is easier and less sensitive than most comparable varieties. Jane Grigson (1982) wrote tellingly of their dangerously bland flavour: 'Victorias are for canning. Victorias are for plums and custard, that crowning moment of the school, hospital, prison and boarding house midday meal: I reflect that Mr Bird invented his powder round about the time that Victoria plums were beginning their career.'

TECHNIQUE:
Plums require shelter from frost and a soil which holds moisture well. Old orchards are on strong rootstocks, giving large trees. Dwarf rootstocks, planted in rows about 6 metres apart are now favoured. Some varieties require pollinators, although Victoria is a variety which is largely self-fertile. Provided the soil is correct, and the land sheltered from frost, plums do well in Kent and its region. After the first 2 years, little maintenance beyond light pruning is carried out.

REGION OF PRODUCTION:
SOUTH EAST ENGLAND, KENT.

Carolina Cheese

DESCRIPTION:
A PRESSED SHEEP'S MILK CHEESE. DIMENSIONS: TRUCKLES APPROXIMATELY 8CM HIGH, 5CM DIAMETER OR 14CM HIGH, 14CM DIAMETER. WEIGHT: ABOUT 750G (SMALL); 2-2.7KG (LARGE). COLOUR: ALMOST WHITE. FLAVOUR: WELL-ROUNDED, WITH A MILD SHEEP NOTE.

HISTORY:
An ancient origin is claimed for the recipe from which these cheeses were evolved: the monks of a Cistercian abbey near Chard, Somerset. This is not impossible; there are parallels in the north of England,

where Wensleydale and related cheeses almost certainly owe their origin to monastic dairy skills.

In its current form, Carolina was developed by John Norman in the Chard area; the name was taken from a field name of land he farmed. In the early 1970s, he began to make a sheep's milk cheese, continuing until ill health prevailed. Ten years later the current maker, Harold Woolley, bought the recipe and transferred production to Kent, where the cheese has been made ever since. He has since evolved 2 similar cheeses – Cecilia (plain and smoked) and Nepicar.

TECHNIQUE:

Carolina, Cecilia and Nepicar are all made from sheep's milk, mostly from Friesland-Romney sheep on permanent pasture. For Carolina, a home-produced starter is incubated overnight and added to the warm milk the next morning followed, about 45 minutes later, by vegetarian rennet. The milk is left for another 45 minutes for the curd to set. The curd is cut, then stirred gently by hand for about 30 minutes, allowed to settle and drained. The curd is cut in blocks and stacked for an hour to drain further. The curd is milled, salted and packed into cloth-lined moulds. The cheeses are pressed individually for 24 hours, being turned once; then they are removed from the moulds, the cloths removed, the cheeses returned to the moulds and pressed a further 24 hours. On removal from the moulds, they are brined for a day. They are matured for 60 days.

Nepicar is made to the same recipe and method, using milk pasteurized by a high-temperature, short-term process, and the cheeses are matured for 90 days. Cecilia is made to a similar recipe, with slight differences in times and temperatures; it is dry-salted rather than brined, and matured in oak barrels over a bed of hops. Frozen milk is stored for use when the sheep stop milking in September.

REGION OF PRODUCTION:

SOUTH EAST ENGLAND, KENT.

Wellington Cheese

DESCRIPTION:

HARD, PRESSED, UNPASTEURIZED COW'S MILK CHEESE IN ROUNDS ABOUT
18CM DIAMETER, 7CM HIGH; A SMALLER ONE IS MADE FOR CHRISTMAS.
WEIGHT: 2.5–3KG (LARGE); 750G (SMALL). COLOUR: A RICH YELLOW WITH
A NATURAL GREY-BROWN MOTTLED RIND. FLAVOUR AND TEXTURE: RICH
CREAMY TEXTURE, VERY SMOOTH; SWEET.

HISTORY:

There is no great history of cheese-making in Berkshire, though
Reading University has latterly been a centre for research into
dairying. Work carried out by the university led to the development of
the recipe for Smallholder Cheese in 1911. It was specifically intended
as a recipe for those wishing to make a hard cheese on a limited scale.
It enjoyed some success with home cheese-makers, still being made at
the end of the 1950s. In the mid-1980s, the maker of Wellington,
Anne Wigmore (a microbiologist at the dairy research institute at the
university) took the Smallholder recipe and developed it for use with
milk from a Guernsey herd kept at Stratfield Saye, the nearby estate
belonging to the Duke of Wellington.

TECHNIQUE:

Unpasteurized milk from one designated herd of Guernsey cattle is
used. The Smallholder recipe is along the following lines. The milk is
heated to 32°C, starter added, followed by vegetarian rennet about 30
minutes later; the top layer is stirred to ensure the cream is mixed in,
then left 40 minutes. The curd is cut 3 ways and allowed to settle. The
heat is increased to 38°C over 30 minutes, the curd stirred continuously,
then the whey is drained off. The curd is cut into strips and stacked and
re-stacked until the correct acidity has developed. Milling is into pieces
the size of a nutmeg; the curd is salted during this process, then filled
into moulds. Pressing is for about 24 hours, the cheese removed from
the mould once (at an early stage) and reversed. The cheeses are
unmoulded and matured 6 months in the cellars at Stratfield Saye.

Anne Wigmore's interest in cheese-making has also led to the development of Spenwood (named after the Berkshire village of Spencer's Wood, where the work was carried out) and Wigmore, both based on sheep's milk; and Waterloo, a soft cow's milk cheese.

REGION OF PRODUCTION:
SOUTH EAST ENGLAND, BERKSHIRE.

Jellied Eels

DESCRIPTION:

A CLEAR JELLY CONTAINING EEL IN PIECES 2–5CM LONG. COLOUR: THE JELLY IS PALE BROWN-GOLD, THE EEL PIECES HAVE LIGHT GREY-BLUE SKIN WITH WHITE FLESH, THE BEST HAVE A FINE PALE BLUE BLOOM ON THE SKIN. FLAVOUR: DELICATE, MILDLY FISHY.

HISTORY:

Eel is a fish once favoured by Cockneys. Thames eels are more silver in colour and sweeter of taste than those from the Continent (Simon, 1960). Among many early recipes, eel pies were celebrated – not least at Eel Pie Island, near Richmond-upon-Thames; Shakespeare describes a Cockney making a pie in *King Lear*, putting eels 'in the paste alive'. Stews and galantines were also made with plenty of eels.

Today eel pie has all but vanished even if the shops seem to keep its name alive, but jellied and stewed eels are still made – sold from street stalls and cooked-food shops in London and seaside towns of Essex and Kent. These are the 'Eel, Pie and Mash' shops, which sell steak and kidney pies, mashed potatoes and cooked eels.

Brian Knights, who has made a study of the eel and its fishery in Britain, observes that eels are now caught in the Thames again. Some of them are used by the jelliers who supply the shops, but imported eels are also employed.

TECHNIQUE:

The eels are kept alive in holding tanks then electrically stunned and killed immediately before use. They are chopped into lengths then boiled for 15–20 minutes in salted water. The eels in their cooking liquor are left to go cold in the large white basins from which they are sold.

REGION OF PRODUCTION:
SOUTH EAST ENGLAND, LONDON.

Oyster

DESCRIPTION:
ENGLISH NATIVE OYSTERS ARE GRADED ACCORDING TO WEIGHT INTO: EXTRA LARGE (OVER 160G); 1: 120–160G; 2: 90–120G; 3: 70–90G. FORM: THE SHELL IS DENSE AND HARD, RELATIVELY FLAT AND SMOOTH, WITH A STRONG NACRE ON THE INSIDE. COLOUR: THE MEAT IS A RICH CREAM, BISCUIT COLOUR.

WHITSTABLE OYSTERS ARE SLOW-GROWING WITH HEAVY SHELLS; THEY MAY WEIGH UP TO 240G AND BE UP TO 11CM LONG.

HISTORY:
The first people to exploit the native oyster, *Ostrea edulis*, on a large scale in this part of Britain were the Romans. The shellfish were even exported to Rome itself (Wilson, 1973). In the Middle Ages, the Colchester fishery was granted a charter in 1189.

There were many other beds of native oysters available to the British, Poole in Dorset and Helford in Cornwall to name but two. Trade between the coasts and consumers inland is documented readily from medieval books of account. But there is little doubt that the most important production was concentrated on the Thames estuary: Colchester on the north side and Whitstable on the south. The 'Company of Free Fishers and Dredgers', an association of oyster fishermen from Whitstable, has a history stretching back over 400 years. At their peak, there were more than 800 principals in the fisheries (Neild, 1995). One reason for their pre-eminence was the existence of London on their doorstep, with easy water transport to link them to Billingsgate, the principal point of sale. One has only to read diaries, correspondence and printed accounts to appreciate the scale of the business. Oysters were an important food of the common people in London: the Mayor regulated the price of oysters from at least the fifteenth century, and an early reference to 'Colchesters' from 1625 confirms the identity of the town with the product.

Oysters were apparently unlimited until a moment in the 1860s. The development of beds off the Sussex coast in the English Channel had caused the price to fall through oversupply, but these were soon exhausted, and disease and a sequence of bad weather combined to cause a shortage elsewhere. The oyster ceased to be food of the masses and became a costly delicacy. Problems first encountered by the Victorians were never properly addressed and the native oyster beds have suffered acute decline in the intervening years. Fears of catching typhoid due to unhygienic storage wiped out demand before the First World War; catastrophic seasons, such as the winter of 1962–3 which killed 95 per cent of marketable stocks; disease; and finally price competition from oyster varieties that were more easily farmed, or more cheaply gathered, were the most potent causes.

Seasalter, the company based in Whitstable which currently does most work on oyster cul-ture in the Thames estuary, has a history which stretches back to the mid-nineteenth century. The fishery of Whitstable did not escape the trials endured by other sites, but recovery has been put in hand. The beds were re-stocked with young natives from other locations, and Pacific oysters were introduced in the 1960s. Both varieties are now farmed at Whitstable. In Colchester, commerce was interrupted by the crises described above, but Colchester Oyster Fishery Ltd was established in 1966 to restore the beds. Stocks were hit badly by the parasite Bonamia in 1982 but are slowly recovering. Whitstable Oysters have been awarded Protected Geographical Indication (PGI).

TECHNIQUE:

Colchester oysters are fattened in the Pyefleet, a creek in the estuary of the River Colne. This is good for the purpose, as it has mildly brackish, nutrient-rich water, containing the phyto-plankton on which oysters thrive. The name 'Pyefleet' has always been jealously guarded by

Colchester Borough Council. The derelict oyster beds at Pyefleet, just south of the town of Colchester, were cleared of accumulated silt in the 1960s, an operation which was followed by natural re-stocking. New storage tanks were built. Water for these is pumped from settlement ponds into a storage pond and filtered into temperature-controlled, oxygenated tanks. The water for holding oysters is circulated through an ultra-violet treatment plant, and the water composition is monitored daily. After purification, the oysters are graded, packed in tubs with seaweed, and distributed.

In Whitstable, native oysters are gathered by a power dredge towed by a trawler which flicks the oysters into a cage; all oysters sold in England are purified in clean water under ultra-violet light for 2 days; after this they are graded by eye. Some farming of native oysters is also carried out at Whitstable, where Pacifics are farmed in mesh bags on steel tables.

To be called a Whitstable oyster, the shellfish must come from the coast between Shoeburyness and North Foreland, north Kent.

REGION OF PRODUCTION:
COLCHESTER (ESSEX); SOUTH EAST ENGLAND, WHITSTABLE (KENT). ALSO EAST ANGLIA.

Patum Peperium

DESCRIPTION:
ANCHOVY RELISH IN SMALL FLAT ROUND PLASTIC BOXES OF 42.5G OR 70G; LARGER GLASS AND PORCELAIN POTS ARE ALSO USED. COLOUR: PINK-BROWN; THE COLOUR OF SALTED ANCHOVY. FLAVOUR: SALTY, FISHY, STRONG ANCHOVY FLAVOUR.

HISTORY:
The recipe for Patum Peperium is said to have been 'perfected' by John Osborn, an English provision merchant living in Paris in 1828. At this time, compounds of fish, meat or cheese, with spices and butter, were very popular. Recipes for potted anchovies, the fish rubbed through a

sieve to remove the bones, mixed with spices and sealed with clarified butter were made and used for garnishes, or spread on toast. The recipe remained the intellectual property of the Osborn family and was brought back to England in the middle of the nineteenth century. According to the company history (Elsenham, n.d.), it was very successful. To the original name, Patum Peperium (the first word appears to be a fanciful play on the word for paste, or pâté; the second is derived from the Greek for pepper), the phrase 'The Gentleman's Relish' was added, apparently by customers asking for the product. Despite the fact that the paste was first made in France, it became closely identified with pre-war British upper-class tastes and remains so today. The brand was sold by the Osborns on the retirement of the last 2 surviving members of the family from the business in 1971.

REGION OF PRODUCTION:
SOUTH EAST ENGLAND, LONDON.

Smoked Salmon (London cure)

DESCRIPTION:
SMOKED WILD SALMON HAS A REDDER HUE THAN THE FARMED, WHICH IS ORANGE-TINTED, AND SLIGHTLY TRANSLUCENT. FLAVOUR AND TEXTURE: SOFT BUTTERY FLAVOUR, VERY MILD SALT AND SMOKE; YIELDING.

HISTORY:
The light London cure developed from a different tradition to those known in Scotland. These last were intended to preserve the fish for a matter of months and were therefore heavy and intrusively flavoured. Immigrants from eastern Europe, arriving in England at the end of the nineteenth century, brought with them expertise in their own style of curing and began to practise in London using supplies of wild salmon from Scotland. The London cure was a means of enhancing flavour rather than of preservation. The fish is intended for consumption within a few hours of processing: it is more mildly flavoured, with a silkier texture than most Scottish smoked salmon.

The most prominent firm, H. Forman and Sons, began curing in 1905. They are the last family firm of East-European origin still working in this field.

TECHNIQUE:
Forman and Sons use both wild and farmed salmon from Scottish waters. The farmed salmon is bought fresh as necessary; the wild is bought in season and supplies are frozen for subsequent use. Much of the fish is smoked to individual orders, the sides selected for size and oil content to the customer's taste. After filleting and trimming, pure salt is used in a very light, dry cure which emphasizes the natural flavour of the fish, rather than masking it as do heavier cures; the sides are then lightly smoked.

REGION OF PRODUCTION:
SOUTH EAST ENGLAND, LONDON.

Whelk

DESCRIPTION:
AT POINT OF SALE, WHELKS ARE DISPLAYED COOKED AND SHELLED; THOSE FROM WHITSTABLE USED FOR THE ENGLISH MARKET GENERALLY WEIGH ABOUT 100–140 PER KG. THE MEAT IS BROWNISH-YELLOW, FLAVOURFUL AND CHEWY; THEY ARE SOLD BY WEIGHT OR IN PRE-WEIGHED PORTIONS. THERE ARE SIGNIFICANT DISPARITIES OF SIZE BETWEEN WHELKS FROM DIFFERENT AREAS AROUND THE BRITISH COAST.

HISTORY:
Whelks, *Buccinum undatum*, are a common gastropod whose coiled, pointed shells are found on the coasts. Variant names are dog whelk, waved whelk, and buckie (in Scotland). The Romans carried them to various inland sites, and they are mentioned in the accounts of fifteenth-century fishmongers and many medieval households. For instance, 4,000 were used to garnish a salted sturgeon at the enthronement of the Archbishop of Canterbury in the early sixteenth

century. The normal medieval procedure was to boil in water and eat with vinegar and parsley (Wilson, 1973).

Fishing grounds for whelks are off the north coast of Norfolk and in the Thames estuary. They formed part of the diet of the London poor, both at home and on holiday on the Kent coast. The phrase, 'he couldn't run a whelk stall', suggests they found a ready sale. However, they were never considered elegant.

When they are bought ready-cooked as street food, the consumer splashes as much vinegar on as he would wish. They remain a seaside staple and as part of the food traditions of the urban poor in Midland cities. The uncooked meat has found a new market in Chinese and Japanese restaurants.

TECHNIQUE:
Whelks are usually fished within a few miles of the shore; the best quality come from open waters. They are carnivorous and plastic barrels or iron baskets baited variously with dead shore crabs, fish offal or salt herring are used to catch them. On the East coast, a number of pots are tied to one rope to form a shank, with a buoy at each end. Weather permitting, the pots are examined, emptied and re-baited daily. Once landed, the fish are boiled in sea-water, shell-on, for 12–16 minutes, then cooled and the meat extracted. The cap (*operculum*) is discarded. Alternatively, some processors crack the shell and remove it, which reduces boiling time to 7–8 minutes. If the whelks are required raw, the shells are crushed and removed before packing.

REGION OF PRODUCTION:
EAST ENGLAND.

Whitebait

DESCRIPTION:
INDIVIDUAL FISH ARE VERY SMALL, 3–4CM IN LENGTH AND SLENDER IN PROPORTION. WEIGHT: TYPICALLY, THERE ARE ABOUT 400 FISH TO A KILO. COLOUR: SEMI-TRANSPARENT, OR SILVER-WHITE. FLAVOUR:

WHITEBAIT ARE VALUED AS MUCH FOR THEIR CRUNCHY TEXTURE AS THEIR FLAVOUR, WHICH, WHILST MILDLY FISHY, IS MASKED BY THE FLAVOUR OF HOT FAT DURING FRYING AND THE LEMON JUICE WITH WHICH MOST PEOPLE SEASON THE DISH JUST BEFORE EATING IT.

HISTORY:

Whitebait may be a mixture of the fry of herring (*Clupea harengus*) and sprat (*Sprattus sprattus*), or the fry of sprat alone. Historians have claimed whitebait first appeared on an English menu as long ago as 1612 (Davidson, 1979). The name derives from the use of these small fish as bait for catching other fish (*OED*). It seems that they really became important as food in the mid-eighteenth century. For at least a century after this time, they were a noted speciality of Blackwall and Greenwich, downstream from the City of London (Mars, 1998).

There was much controversy over the exact nature of whitebait, some claiming that it was actually a separate species. This debate was still alive in 1861 when Mrs Beeton stated, 'This highly esteemed little fish appears in innumerable multitudes in the river Thames, near Greenwich and Blackwall, during the month of July, when it forms a tempting dish to vast numbers of Londoners who flock to the various taverns of these places in order to gratify their appetites ... The ministers of the Crown have had a custom, for many years, of having a "whitebait dinner" just before the close of the session.' This ministerial dinner has origins more banal than epicurean delight in fish fry. There used once to be an annual shindig held at Dagenham by the commissioners for embanking the River Thames. To one of these, in the 1790s, Pitt the Younger was invited and brought some of his Cabinet colleagues. The habit stuck but the location was shifted to the more salubrious Greenwich in the early part of the next century. Only then did they start to eat whitebait. The tradition continued until 1894.

Whitebait still shoal in the mouth of the Thames but the fishery has declined. According to one of the few remaining fishermen, demand for the fish has dropped, partly because they are cooked by deep-frying, now considered an unhealthy method, and because

The South East

imported whitebait are cheaper than fish caught locally, due to the way in which the fishing industries of other countries are subsidized.

The fishing of whitebait is no longer encouraged because of the implications for fish stocks, though the sprat is not under any threat at present. A whitebait festival was held annually at Southend, down the estuary, at the same time as a ceremony of blessing the sea.

TECHNIQUE:
Whitebait were defined by Alan Davidson (1979) as 'the fry of various clupeoid fish, notably the herring and the sprat, and often mixed together'; most authorities now state that they are the fry of the sprat alone. They are caught from boats working in pairs with a fine net stretched between them. The season was considered to be March–August, but now fishing is discouraged when there are immature fish in the river, a period which lasts approximately from June until October.

REGION OF PRODUCTION:
SOUTH EAST ENGLAND.

Aylesbury Duck

DESCRIPTION:
OVEN-READY WEIGHT, 3.5–4KG. WHITE FEATHERS AND PINK BEAK; THE FLESH IS PALE, SOFT AND TENDER, WITH LITTLE GRAIN AND LESS FATTY THAN MOST DUCK TYPES; THE FAT IS LOCATED IN A THIN HARD LAYER UNDER THE SKIN. FLAVOUR IS GOOD, WITH PRONOUNCED GAMINESS.

HISTORY:
The family of the one remaining commercial producer has been rearing Aylesbury ducks since the last quarter of the eighteenth century. Martha Bradley, writing in 1756, thought any breed of duck acceptable for the table, but by the time of Mrs Beeton (1861), Aylesburys were noted for their excellence and the intensive system of rearing then current: 'not on plains or commons … but in the abodes of the cottagers. Round the walls of the living-rooms, and of the bedroom

even, are fixed rows of wooden boxes, lined with hay; and it is the business of the wife and children to nurse and comfort the feathered lodgers, to feed the little ducklings, and to take the old ones out for an airing. Sometimes the "stock" ducks are the cottager's own property, but it more frequently happens that they are intrusted to his care by a wholesale breeder who pays him so much per score for all ducklings properly raised.' Transport was a factor in the fame of the birds; Smithfield, the London wholesale meat market, was easily accessible.

The old system of rearing died out before the First World War; at the same time, hybrid ducks with Chinese blood became common. The popularity of the Aylesbury declined in the face of competition from birds of more acceptable conformation. Strict enforcement of EU hygiene regulations have further reduced the number of duck-farmers by vastly reducing the economic viability of the business for small producers.

TECHNIQUE:
The ducklings are now hatched in incubators. They are kept indoors for the first 2 weeks of life, and then allowed access to the open air in fenced runs for the third. After this, they are kept in outdoor enclosures for about 5 weeks. For the first 3 weeks they subsist on a high-protein ration; feeding of this continues once they are outdoors, but they also forage for grass and insects. The ducklings are killed at 8 weeks; they are dry-plucked, waxed, and hung 48 hours before evisceration and trussing. Older ducks of a larger size and more mature flavour are available when the breeding stock is killed at about 14 months.

REGION OF PRODUCTION:
SOUTH EAST ENGLAND, BUCKINGHAMSHIRE.

Romney Sheep

DESCRIPTION:
ABOUT 18–20KG DRESSED WEIGHT FOR A CARCASS AT 3–4 MONTHS; 25KG LATER IN SEASON. HEAVY-BODIED SHEEP WITH GOOD CONFORMATION. MEAT IS DARK, WELL-FLAVOURED, CLOSE-TEXTURED.

Romneys are white-faced, naturally long-tailed, and related to the Cheviot, Ile de France, Texel and Welsh Mountain. Their name is that of their native district, Romney Marsh. The stock which may have given rise to the breed were imported in about the second century AD by the Romans. Large numbers of sheep were maintained at Romney by the medieval Priory of Canterbury – whose breeding flock was at Thanet – for the sake of their wool, milk and meat. The relative importance of these products to the strain has waxed and waned. At present it is primarily a wool sheep. In the past, they were shorn of wool in the summer of their birth and sold as store lambs to be finished by arable farmers, graziers and butchers. They were slaughtered for meat as hoggets (over a year old). Often they were kept to 2 years, by which time they became very fat.

The Romney was mentioned by Youatt (1837) as crossed with the Southdown, popular further along the coast. The progeny was suited to meat production. The Kent and Romney Marsh Sheep Breeders Association was founded in 1895 and the breed has been much exported.

TECHNIQUE:

The owners of the sheep used to live around the edge of the marsh and paid 'lookers' (people from the marsh itself who could tolerate the brackish well-water and the malarial fevers) to oversee the sheep. Before modern veterinary treatments for parasitic infections, managing the flocks to avoid infestation was skilled.

Romneys can be kept in large flocks and they scatter whilst grazing. Some still graze long-established native pastures on which grass species include perennial rye grass and Kentish wild white clover – which can be very close grazed. The pastures were kept close-cropped by moving the sheep frequently. There is a tradition of moving the ewes to arable land in Surrey and Sussex during the winter to feed on root crops, although nowadays they may be housed indoors on their home farms. The object is to allow an early flush of grass on summer pastures.

The lambs are born outdoors, traditionally from 1 April onwards.

They are slaughtered from 3–4 months. Romney lamb reared on the salt marshes is sometimes requested by butchers or restaurants and the breed society has taken an interest in this in the past. However, the British consumer was not willing to pay a premium for the extra flavour, so it was not actively promoted. Romneys are still occasionally crossed with Southdowns to produce lambs for meat, but other lowland breeds such as Suffolk and, lately, Texel, have been favoured.

REGION OF PRODUCTION:
SOUTH EAST ENGLAND.

Southdown Sheep

DESCRIPTION:
DRESSED CARCASS WEIGHT IS ABOUT 17KG. A COMPACT, FLESHY SHEEP WITH FINE BONES AND A HIGH RATIO OF MEAT TO BONE; EXCELLENT, SWEET FLAVOUR, GOOD MARBLING, VERY JUICY.

HISTORY:
The sheep collectively known as 'down' breeds evolved from the native stock of the chalk hills of southern England. This area has been sheep-raising country for many centuries and, by the 1700s, several distinct races had evolved. The first to receive any attention was the South-down. Improvements were begun by John Ellman of Glynde (Sussex). Thereafter, it was considered one of the best producers of lamb and mutton. Mrs Beeton (1861) comments on the 'recent improvements', and remarks, 'of all mutton, that furnished by the Southdown sheep is most highly esteemed; it is also the dearest on account of its scarcity, and the great demand for it.'

'From the beginning of the nineteenth century, the fashionable Southdown was increasingly interbred with all the downland breeds and this transformed them,' thus the origin of Oxford Down, Hampshire Down, and Dorset Down (Hall & Clutton-Brock, 1989). It was also used to improve the Shropshire and bred with the Norfolk to produce the ancestors of the modern Suffolk – now much used for meat.

The Downs consist of several relatively high chalk escarpments with steep faces and dry valleys; the flora is typified by soft, short turf with a great diversity of herbs and flowering plants. Sheep grazing, a part of the area's economy since the Middle Ages, is a vital element in its maintenance. In the nineteenth century, the Southdown was of enormous importance to Sussex farms which practised a system of folding the flocks on arable crops at night with extensive grazing on the short, downland pasture during the day. This survived until recently in a few places. Its drawbacks are that it is labour intensive and less ploughland is now available, partly because of set-aside. Many Southdown sheep are now kept on ley pasture.

Lambing usually begins in February. They are sold for meat from about 16 weeks but many are retained for breeding; Southdown rams are in demand as sires for cross-bred lambs. The value of these has been recognized for well over 150 years, when Mrs Beeton remarked that Southdown crossed with Lincoln or Leicester were used to supply the London meat markets; the crossing breeds may have changed to Cluns, Cotswolds and Dartmoors, but the principle remains the same. A premium is often paid for Southdown lambs; demand is high and there is much direct marketing.

REGION OF PRODUCTION:
SOUTH EAST ENGLAND, SUSSEX.

Sussex Cattle

DESCRIPTION:
SUSSEX PROVIDE COMPACT, FINE-BONED CARCASSES WHICH HAVE A DRESSED WEIGHT OF 250–272KG. THE FLESH HAS AN EXCELLENT, SWEET FLAVOUR; WELL-MARBLED WITH A FINE GRAIN, EXTREMELY TENDER.

HISTORY:
Sussex cattle have red-brown pelts, a characteristic dating back many centuries. Red cattle in the county are mentioned in the Domesday Book

(1086). The breed developed from draught oxen (a use which continued into the early 1900s). They were worked for several years before slaughter for beef. By the nineteenth century, they were recognized as fine beef animals. Registration of pedigree began in the mid-Victorian period and the breed society was founded in the 1870s. Sussex have been much exported, especially for beef production in southern Africa.

TECHNIQUE:

The breed has developed to give a hardy foraging animal, capable of remaining outside all year. In practice, this only happens on the chalk downs where the soils are light and thin; on lower ground, the cattle are housed for the first 3 months of the year to prevent the grassland, which overlies heavy clay soils, being poached. Housed cattle are fed hay, silage and straw and little, if any, concentrate. Animals in fruit-growing areas may be given the excess apples and pears in the autumn. The land on which the animals graze for much of the year includes the long-established and herb-rich grasslands of the chalk downs. Sussex cattle are also kept in the harsh micro-climate of Isle of Sheppey. This place, with a relatively low annual rainfall and exposed to cold north-easterly winds, is categorized as a Site of Special Scientific Interest; consequently restrictions are imposed affecting the date at which the grass can be cut for hay (1 July) and the use of fertilizers, maintaining a unique flora. Calving is arranged to take place in spring or autumn; the calves are suckled until weaning. They are killed at 18–24 months. Whilst some pure-bred Sussex beef reaches the market, the cattle are also crossed with continental breeds to produce large, lean, commercial carcasses.

REGION OF PRODUCTION:
SOUTH EAST ENGLAND.

Sussex Chicken

DESCRIPTION:

A HEAVY BIRD (ABOUT 3KG DRESSED WEIGHT AT 16–20 WEEKS) WITH A BROAD BREAST. WELL-FLAVOURED, WHITE FLESH WITH A JUICY,

SUCCULENT TEXTURE. THERE ARE SEVERAL VARIETIES DISTINGUISHED BY THE COLOUR OF THEIR PLUMAGE, WITH PALE FEATHERS GENERALLY BEING FAVOURED IN THE LAST 100 YEARS.

HISTORY:

The history of poultry – for meat or for eggs – is not especially long or glorious in Britain. It was a matter of the barn-door fowl and the farmer's wife tending a small flock, with little specialization or arcane skill. Cookery books often contained instruction on fattening or cramming, but the almost sacerdotal tending of birds for the table undertaken in France or Belgium was not at first widespread in this country. The agriculturalist William Marshall (1796) noticed that none of the poultry of Devon was shut up at night or in any way confined so as to harvest the egg crop. At that time, the district around Berwick-upon-Tweed (Northumbria) was an important source of eggs for the London market. Scottish routines for extending the laying day were more advanced than those of the South-West. Indeed, it was only at the beginning of the twentieth century that a market for 'fresh-laid' eggs was identifiable in any way. More than 2 billion eggs were imported into Britain in the year 1900, some from as far away as Eastern Europe – hardly fresh.

There was no great distinction between breeds of British chicken until the nineteenth century and most of those that were distinguished were of foreign origin. Hence, the Poland was Dutch and the Cochin was from Shanghai, to name two that commanded remarkable prices for their ornamental value. Two varieties represented indigenous English stock: Indian Game and the Dorking. The Dorking fowl was unique in having 5 toes. Its flesh was white, and it was the most famous table bird produced for the London market. There were other Surrey varieties, all related (but none having the extra toes), and this is indication enough that the existence of a large market stimulated the development of breeds specific to its requirements. At the first Poultry Breeders' Show, held in London in 1845, there were classes for Dorkings, Surrey, Kent and Old Sussex fowls.

The Dorking's origins have been pushed back to the time of the Roman occupation, in myth at least. The Roman agricultural writer Columella did indeed give a description of a five-toed bird which closely resembles it in colour and form. A thousand years later, the early history of the race and its place of origin were still in dispute between the poultrymen of Sussex and Surrey: each county claiming to be the motherland. The facts have never been capable of resolution and the likelihood is a common source for most South-Eastern birds. As London spread over the Surrey hills, so the rearing and fattening of fowl extended towards the county of Sussex, particularly the area around Heathfield. There arose a Sussex system of cramming, with oats ground between millstones tooled for the purpose, mixed with hog's grease, sugar and milk – this survived until 1939–45. Not all the birds so fattened were of Dorking, Surrey or Sussex descent. Many were imported from Ireland for finishing closer to the point of sale. The fatteners also surgically caponized some of their flock to produce the famous 'Surrey Capons'.

A breeders' club for Sussex chickens was formed in 1903 and three varieties – light, speckled and red – were standardized. Other plumage colours, some gender-linked, have been developed over the years. The Sussex has also been much crossed with other varieties of British chickens. It was used with the Indian Game (which, despite its name, has been bred in Britain for centuries) in the 1930s to develop the Ixworth, a bird which has been neglected commercially despite having excellent qualities.

The impact of the Second World War on food production in general and the introduction of commercial broiler-chicken systems from the USA started a decline in traditional poultry farming which is not yet arrested.

TECHNIQUE:

A few specialist breeders still keep Sussex fowl. The poultry farms of the past, using caponizing and cramming, have died out and are unlikely to be ever reintroduced; and the casual system in which poultry ranged freely under the care of the farmer's wife, who collected the eggs and dressed table poultry for the market, is on the verge of extinction. The concern of those who now keep Sussex strains is as much to preserve bloodlines and genetic diversity as to produce eggs and meat. Because of this and because of the costs involved in rearing the fowl, they are usually kept under close supervision and a system of fold units, or coops with runs on grass enclosed by wire mesh, is followed. Each unit, containing one cockerel and several hens, is moved daily to allow access to fresh grass. Supplementary feed of protein pellets and grain is given daily. The chickens, hatched in spring, are marked to identify the genetic strain, particularly important in flocks which are kept closed – at least one has been in existence since the 1930s.

All poultry breeders who wish to market their birds as meat now have to observe strictly enforced regulations of hygiene and slaughter, requiring the use of an accredited abattoir. There are relatively few of these. The slaughter-houses are obliged to concentrate on one species of meat animal on any given day, and generally prefer to operate with large throughputs. These factors, added to high transport costs, have had an adverse effect on small poultry breeders.

REGION OF PRODUCTION:
SOUTH EAST ENGLAND.

Chelsea Bun

DESCRIPTION:
A LOOSE SPIRAL BUN, SQUARED OFF AT THE SIDES; APPROXIMATELY 100MM SQUARE BY 40MM DEEP. WEIGHT: 100–120G. COLOUR: GOLD-BROWN ON TOP WHERE WELL-BAKED, FADING TO PALE CREAM AT THE SIDES WHERE THE BUNS HAVE TOUCHED. FLAVOUR: SWEET, LIGHTLY SPICED, WITH DRIED FRUIT.

HISTORY:
Chelsea buns have been known since the eighteenth century. Originally they were sold from a pastry cook's shop known as the Bun House in Chelsea. David (1977) discusses the history of the buns and

the Bun House, and speculates that the patronage of the royal family in the 1730s may have helped their popularity. Their earliest occurrence in literature is 1711, when Jonathan Swift reported buying one for a penny and finding that it was stale (*OED*).

The Chelsea bun as made at the Bun House was thought very light, rich and delicate in the early 1800s, but there is no record of what size or shape they were; it can only be assumed that they were the coils we now associate with them. The Bun House in Pimlico Road was demolished in 1839. Kirkland (1907) said that it was 'a popular bun in English confectioners' shops – but, it must be confessed, not so popular as it was at one time.' Observations by Harris and Borella (*c.* 1900) show there were various grades baked, and that bakers did not view Chelsea buns with much regard, a situation which has continued through the century. They are to be found in many bakers' shops and are generally rather large and filling.

TECHNIQUE:

A ferment of milk, sugar, yeast and flour is set. A small proportion of butter is rubbed into the rest of the flour, the ferment is whisked with eggs and more sugar and added to the dough. Once fermented, the dough is rolled into square sheets and the surface brushed with melted butter; brown sugar, mixed with cinnamon or spices, is strewn over the surface, followed by a scatter of currants; then the whole is rolled up and cut in slices about 30mm deep. These are placed cut side down on a greased sheet. The spacing is crucial for, as the buns prove and spread, each should touch its neighbour to give the signature square shape. While still hot from the oven, the buns are glazed with milk and sugar and sometimes dusted with caster sugar. An icing of water and powdered sugar may be used instead of a glaze.

REGION OF PRODUCTION:
SOUTH EAST ENGLAND, LONDON.

The South East

Huffkin

DESCRIPTION:

A FLATTISH, CIRCULAR ROLL WITH A DIMPLE IN THE CENTRE, 150MM DIAMETER, 20MM DEEP. WEIGHT: 80–90G. COLOUR AND TEXTURE: PALE CRUST, WHITE CRUMB, LIGHT OPEN TEXTURE, SMOOTH THIN CRUST.

HISTORY:

Florence White (1932) remarked that huffkins (hufkins or uffkins) were particularly associated with east Kent. She described them as 'thick flat oval cakes of light bread with a hole in the middle'. They have been known since at least 1790. Joseph Wright (1896–1905) cites a quotation from this date. A contributor to *Notes & Queries* (1869) expresses it well: 'Most people know what muffins and crumpets are, but in East Kent … the former are known as uffkins.' Manufacture seems to have declined greatly since World War II; in 1978 David Mabey stated that huffkins had all but disappeared. David Hopper, whose family have been bakers in north-east Kent for several generations, bears this out, but affirms they are still seen occasionally.

TECHNIQUE:

Old recipes show them to be made from a simple flour, water and yeast dough with a little lard, usually in between one-eighth and one-twelfth the quantity of flour. This was kneaded into the dough after the first rise. Spicer (1948) proposes an alternative strategy of melting the lard with hot water at the outset of mixing the dough. After baking, the huffkins are wrapped in a cloth to prevent the crust from hardening. Modern commercial recipes include sugar and milk powder.

REGION OF PRODUCTION:

SOUTH EAST ENGLAND, KENT.

Bread Pudding

DESCRIPTION:

BREAD PUDDING IS BAKED IN LARGE, SHALLOW, SQUARE TRAYS AND SOLD IN INDIVIDUAL PORTIONS MEASURING ABOUT 750MM SQUARE, 250MM DEEP AND WEIGHING ABOUT 150G. COLOUR: IRREGULAR GOLD-BEIGE; THICKLY SPRINKLED WITH CASTER SUGAR. FLAVOUR AND TEXTURE: DENSE, MOIST AND SWEET, WITH SPICES AND DRIED FRUIT.

HISTORY:

This pudding is one English response to the problem of what to do with leftovers. There are others, such as bread-and-butter pudding (layering thin slices of buttered bread with custard) or Poor Knights of Windsor (deep-frying the slices and serving them with sugar); but bread pudding is the only one which has much history of commercialization. How long it has been sold in the South-East, however, is unknown. The idea can be traced back several centuries. John Nott (1726) gives 3 recipes for puddings based on bread, including one, 'Grateful Pudding', which shares some elements of the modern form, including the additions of eggs and dried fruit, the resulting batter being baked in a dish and served dusted with sugar. Hannah Glasse (1747) gave several, ranging from extremely rich to quite plain. Maria Rundell (1807) included a good selection, with a plainer one requiring suet rather than butter and cream. Mrs Beeton's (1861) are notably spare: the cream has vanished, the butter diminished, and suet more important.

This appears to be a turning point in the history of the product. The essential details of soaked bread mixed with sugar, fat, spice and fruit, poured into a dish and baked are all there, but the more delicate recipes known in the eighteenth century vanish.

TECHNIQUE:

Modern recipes for bread pudding are unsophisticated. Stale bread (baker's bread, not the sliced, white, moist, plastic-wrapped loaves from industrial plant bakeries) is required. This is soaked in water overnight. The water is drained, the bread squeezed dry by hand. The bread is measured, usually by volume, to establish the quantity of other ingredients required, principally suet, sugar and dried fruit which are each added in quantities of one-third the volume of soaked bread. These are mixed into the bread together with a little spice ('mixed' sweet spice – clove, allspice and cinnamon – is the usual choice); sometimes a little flour is added. This is made into a batter by the addition of milk and eggs and baked.

REGION OF PRODUCTION:
SOUTH EAST ENGLAND.

Ginger Cake

DESCRIPTION:
COLOUR: A VERY DARK RICH BROWN. FLAVOUR: SWEET, WITH BITTER MOLASSES NOTE AND DISTINCT GINGER.

HISTORY:

Ginger cakes are known all over Britain but there is markedly less interest in them in the North and West where there are already distinctive gingerbreads with a strong local following. Ginger has long been an important baking spice in Europe, where it was often associated (as were other spices) with fairings and celebration. The cake described here is a continuation and development of that tradition but peculiar to Britain.

In the 1840s, the *Magazine of Domestic Economy* noted that in London the manufacture of gingerbread was very important, and that it was made into long narrow cakes to export to India. It was based on flour, treacle and ginger, and the author considered that other ingredients added were 'mere supernumeraries imparting flavour and they may therefore be varied at will'. Butter, egg whites, and a leavening of ammonia salts are mentioned in this context. This is the ancestor of modern ginger cakes. A richer, more refined ginger cake, using sugar rather than treacle, is mentioned in the same article. Flour and treacle gingerbread has vanished, but rich ginger cakes are still made by domestic and craft bakers. Their methods are heavily influenced by the nineteenth-century developments in bakery techniques which allowed quick and easy leavening (baking powders) and light sweetening (sugars).

TECHNIQUE:

Ginger cakes are enriched with butter, vegetable fat or lard, and eggs; bicarbonate of soda or baking powder is favoured as leavening agent. Black treacle and Golden Syrup are usually added. The proportions of flour, fat and sugar are 2:1:1, and the weight of black treacle added is usually about three-quarters the weight of sugar. Other ingredients may include chopped candied peel, dried fruit, apple pieces, or chunks of preserved ginger.

REGION OF PRODUCTION:

SOUTH EAST ENGLAND.

Maids Of Honour

DESCRIPTION:

A ROUND OPEN TART, 80MM DIAMETER, 35MM DEEP. WEIGHT: ABOUT 60G. COLOUR: LIGHT BROWN PASTRY, YELLOW FILLING, GOLDEN IN PATCHES. FLAVOUR: SWEET, RICH, ALMONDS.

HISTORY:

These little tarts are of a type widespread in the past but now rare. They resemble simple cheesecakes. The name is first used in the middle of the eighteenth century. It is possible it derives from the close connections of the royal court with the former palace of Richmond (in which town they appear first to have been made), or with the palace at Kew (now the Royal Botanic Gardens) purchased by Frederick, Prince of Wales and long the home of his son King George III. The recipe in use today in 'The Original Maids of Honour Shop' opposite the walls of Kew Gardens came into the hands of the Newens family, the present owners, in the mid-nineteenth century when an ancestor served an apprenticeship at the Richmond Maids of Honour shop. Production continued in both Richmond and the adjacent village of Kew, but it is in the latter place that the pastries are now made. Other bakers produce variations, but none is authentic. Newens Maids of Honour is a trademark.

TECHNIQUE:

The recipe is a trade secret. Puff pastry is always used for the case and the filling consists of a mixture of milk, breadcrumbs, butter, sugar, grated lemon rind, ground almonds and eggs. The objective is a very well-risen, crisp case filled with a moist, lightly browned filling.

REGION OF PRODUCTION:

SOUTH EAST ENGLAND, KEW (SURREY).

Bittermints

DESCRIPTION:

A SMALL, THICK, DISC 45MM DIAMETER, 9MM DEEP. WEIGHT: 18G. COLOUR: VERY DARK CHOCOLATE COATING, WITH WHITE FONDANT CENTRE. FLAVOUR: THE CHOCOLATE IS BITTER, THE FONDANT POWERFULLY FLAVOURED WITH MINT. COMPOSITION: CHOCOLATE, SUGAR, MINT. BITTERMINTS ARE LARGE, WITH A LOW SUGAR CONTENT IN THE COATING AND A STRENGTH OF MINT FLAVOUR CONTRASTING MARKEDLY WITH SIMILAR PRODUCTS WHICH ARE MOSTLY SMALLER AND INVARIABLY SWEETER.

HISTORY:

Mint has been used as a flavour for grained-sugar sweets in Britain since at least the early 1800s. In 1830, a provincial confectioner S.W. Stavely told his readers how to make candied peppermint. Sugar fondant became popular as a filling for chocolate confectionery about 50 years later. In *The Complete Confectioner* (*c*. 1910) Skuse commented, while giving a recipe for peppermint cream patties, that 'the fondant cream has been of great assistance to the cocoa bean in providing luscious centres'. In 1921, Lousia Thorpe suggested peppermint creams could be coated with chocolate, although she was unlikely to be the first person to have the idea. It was about then that

Colonel Benson and Mr Dickinson established 'Bendicks', a chocolatier's, in Mayfair, London. Bittermints were created in 1931. The recipe remains unchanged, and is regarded as the quintessential British mint. No other firm uses the name.

TECHNIQUE:

An unblended mint oil from the American West Coast is specified for the fondant; a relatively high percentage is added. The chocolate is made from a blend of cocoa beans, roasted and refined to produce cocoa liquor of distinctive character; it has an unusually coarse texture. The mint centre is double-coated with the chocolate.

REGION OF PRODUCTION:
SOUTH EAST ENGLAND.

Bitter Beer (Kent)

DESCRIPTION:

THE COLOUR IS FROM TAWNY-GOLD TO COPPERY RED. THE TASTE HAS A HOPPY AND BITTER FINISH TINGED WITH SWEETNESS. ALCOHOL BY VOLUME IS 3.4–5.2 PER CENT.

HISTORY:

Kent was famed as early as the twelfth century for producing the finest ale in England (Wilson, 1973). This was ale in the Old English sense, a fermented drink made from malt without hops, which were unknown in Britain until their introduction in the 1500s by Flemish settlers in this very county.

Hops gradually replaced the other herbs and spices which had been used to flavour beer. They had the double advantage of tasting pleasant and acting as a preservative. They give the bitter note and thus the name to the most widely-drunk beer style. Kent remains a centre of cultivation, with hop gardens and oast houses a feature of the landscape. The freshness of the hops available to brewers in Kent gives distinctive flavour and character to their beer.

Shepherd Neame at Faversham in Kent was founded in the last

years of the seventeenth century. It has since been in continuous production: longer than any other in the country.

TECHNIQUE:

Technique does not differ from other British beers. Shepherd Neame makes its strongest bitter (Bishop's Finger) with a mash of crushed malt and liquor drawn from the company's own well bored into an aquifer in the greensand stratum. The wort is strained off into a brew kettle and boiled with Target, Challenger and Goldings hops (all local) for 60–90 minutes. A proportion of the hops is added towards the end of the boil; the wort is strained and cooled and the company's own yeast strain added. Fermentation is for 7 days; more hops are added to ale intended for casks. It is racked into conventional casks to stand for 3–4 days before distribution. If it is to be bottled, it is first filtered and pasteurized. Kentish Ale and Kentish Strong Ale have been awarded Protected Geographical Indication (PGI).

REGION OF PRODUCTION:
SOUTH EAST ENGLAND.

Flag Porter

DESCRIPTION:

IN APPEARANCE, A DEEP MAHOGANY WITH A CREAMY HEAD AND FINE BUBBLES. ITS FLAVOUR IS AROMATIC, SWEETISH, WITH CHARACTERISTIC TOASTED AND FRUITED UNDERTONES. IT IS 5 PER CENT ALCOHOL BY VOLUME.

HISTORY:

Porter and stout owe their distinctive qualities to London water. Jackson (1993) suggests they may have become so closely associated with London and Dublin (Guinness) because the waters of these cities did not lend themselves to the paler beers that became fashionable in the late nineteenth century. Wilson (1973) remarks that by the reign of Elizabeth I, London ale already had a good reputation. The word porter, applied to beer, seems in the mid-eighteenth century to have meant porters' ale, i.e. a beer drunk by porters and other labourers. Quotations from this period attribute its invention to a brewer in Shoreditch in 1722. His beer was called 'entire' because it is said to have included the characteristics of 3 contemporary beer styles, normally mixed in the jug by drawing from different barrels. Originally, the word 'porter' covered several strengths and weights, but then the fuller- bodied 'stouter' examples appear to have become a style in their own right – the modern stout (Jackson, 1993).

A high-temperature roasting process, essential for the malt for these dark beers, was patented in 1817; the grains were roasted in a rotating drum so they could be exposed to the higher temperatures without being burned. Porter was stored in large wooden tuns, giving microflora which lent a characteristic smell.

Porter went out of fashion in the British Isles during the 1960s and production almost ceased, but it was revived in the 1970s and is now popular again. One brand, Flag Porter, is brewed to a nineteenth-century recipe. The yeast for the brew was recovered from sealed bottles found in a ship wrecked in 1825 in the English Channel, and cultured for use in the beer. It is probably the closest in style to the porter of Georgian London. Flag Porter is made by Elgood's in Wisbech, Cambridgeshire; Young's, an old-established London company, still brew a porter in London itself; others make porter-style beers.

TECHNIQUE:

Flag Porter is based on a Whitbread recipe from the mid-nineteenth century. The barley and hops used are grown without pesticides or chemical fertilizers. It is made from pale, crystal, brown and chocolate malts, with Fuggles hops, by the conventional English brewing method. The primary fermentation uses top-fermenting modern yeast; a secondary fermentation uses yeast cultured from the Channel wreck. The beer is then fined, pasteurized and bottled.

REGION OF PRODUCTION:

SOUTH EAST ENGLAND.

Imperial Russian Stout

DESCRIPTION:

THIS STOUT IS ALMOST BLACK, WITH RED GLINTS. ITS FLAVOUR IS VERY COMPLEX, WITH ELEMENTS OF ROASTED, SMOKY, TAR-LIKE FLAVOURS AND BURNT CURRANTS. IT IS GENERALLY 9.5–10.5 PER CENT ALCOHOL BY VOLUME, ALTHOUGH SOME ARE ONLY 7 PER CENT.

HISTORY:

Stout evolved alongside porter as a type of dark beer in eighteenth-century England. Whilst the currency of porter declined, several stouts remained as specialities. One was Imperial Stout, an allusion to its popularity in Tsarist Russia (Jackson, 1993). At least 10 London breweries made this style, particularly in Southwark. From here the beer was shipped to Bremen and the Baltic ports. One of these breweries is now owned by the Courage group which shifted production to John Smith's Brewery, Tadcaster, Yorkshire, despite the London association. Like most dark beers, it is more favoured as a winter drink. Another version, called Vassilinsky's Black Russian Beer, is made by McMullen's, Hertford. There is a third, also brewed in Tadcaster, but by Samuel, not John, Smith's.

TECHNIQUE:

Brewing Imperial Russian stout at the Courage brewery commences with a mash of pale ale, amber and black malts, plus a proportion of Pilsner malt (included in the recipe since the nineteenth century). The wort is boiled in a brew kettle with Targets hops. Fermentation is at 23–24°C for 5–6 days, using top-fermenting yeast. There follow 2 weeks of warm conditioning in the fermentation tank, then removal to a second tank for several weeks to condition further. Bottling is carried out without filtration or pasteurization. Originally, the beer was kept for 18 months–2 years before being released.

Samuel Smith's brews its Imperial Stout with crystal malts and roasted barley, using the Yorkshire squares method of fermentation, allowing about 24 hours longer than standard bitter for the stout to ferment.

Sloe Gin

DESCRIPTION:

SLOE GIN IS A DEEP, CLEAR RED. IT HAS A RICH, SLIGHTLY BITTER PLUM FLAVOUR.

HISTORY:

From the start of distilling in Britain at the end of the Middle Ages, crude spirits were rectified to eliminate undesirable flavours by redistilling with ingredients such as aniseed before being sweetened and coloured. Alternatively, a good-quality spirit was used to make a cordial by steeping with flavourings like apricot kernels. This set a precedent. During the eighteenth century, many British towns had distilleries to make gin, then a popular new drink. London dry gin is now made by taking a neutral alcohol (triple-distilled through a rectifying still), adding a mixture of 'botanicals' (flavourings such as juniper berries, citrus peels, etc.) and distilling again.

Sloes are a type of wild plum, the fruit of the blackthorn (*Prunus spinosa*) which is native to Britain and grows in hedges and scrubby woodland. An early literary reference to sloe-flavoured gin dates from the 1890s, although 'sloe-juice negus' is mentioned 50 years earlier. It is probable that country people have used sloes as flavouring for many centuries (*OED*). André Simon (1960) calls sloe gin 'one of the oldest and best English liqueurs'. Mabey (1978) states that distiller Thomas Grant, working in Kent in the mid-nineteenth century, made early experiments with sloe gin on a commercial scale. Hugh Williams, the master-distiller for Gordon's Gin, comments that the recipe used by his company is over 150 years old.

TECHNIQUE:

The domestic method requires sloes mixed with gin and sugar – some recipes also call for a few bitter almonds. It is often recommended that the sloes be left on the trees until after the first frosts, which damage the skin slightly, helping release the flavour. The mixture is steeped for about 3 months, stirred occasionally and strained; the gin is bottled and allowed to mature. Damsons can be used in the same way.

Sloe gin is made commercially by Gordon's to a method developed from this: the sloes are frozen and the gin poured over them. They are left to macerate for about 4 weeks before the liquid is drawn off. Demineralized water is added to the residue to extract alcohol absorbed by the sloes, as well as a little more colour and flavour. This is also strained off, and the liquids are mixed and left for 10 days for sediment to precipitate. The batch is filtered and bottled.

Two other brands of sloe gin available are 'Hawkers' and 'Lamplight'. At least one is made by a method requiring the addition of essences.

REGION OF PRODUCTION:
SOUTH EAST ENGLAND.

Anchovy Sauce

HISTORY:
This is a store sauce, a long-keeping concoction of various flavourings. Anchovies have always been used to enrich gravies and sauces. The origin of the modern sauce may lie in 'cullis' (French *coulis*), a strong broth of meat or fish (often anchovy), herbs, spices, vinegars or wines for thickening and flavouring all sorts of ragouts and soups.

It was a logical step to develop a compound based on anchovy which kept well and could be added to food as required. It is probably more correct to call them ketchups or essences; they should not be confused with fresh sauces flavoured with anchovy sent to table. These essences were first commercialized in the late eighteenth or early nineteenth centuries. An early success was 'Lazenbys Anchovy Essence' (Wilson, 1973). Dr Kitchiner (1817) gives recipes, comments on adulteration and imitation of these products, and quotes prices for them. Bottled anchovy essences have been in production ever since. Although anchovies are occasionally caught off the British coast, the salted fish have been imported from the Mediterranean since the sixteenth century and, because of the quantities required, must always have been used for making essences.

TECHNIQUE:

Modern ingredients are listed as anchovies, salt, xanthan gum, spices, and colouring (E162). The method is a trade secret but is no more complex than pounding the fish in water, simmering with seasonings (including cayenne and mace) and rubbing through a sieve (*Law's Grocer's Manual, c.* 1895). Colouring has long been used: bole Armeniac (a reddish, astringent clay formerly imported from Armenia) in the past, now replaced by extract of beetroot. Early recipes show the essence was usually thickened with flour; gum now has this function.

REGION OF PRODUCTION:

SOUTH EAST ENGLAND

Chelsea Physic Garden Honey

DESCRIPTION:

THIS IS A MEDIUM-COLOURED, AROMATIC, POLYFLORAL HONEY WHICH REMAINS LIQUID FOR ABOUT 5 MONTHS AFTER REMOVAL FROM THE COMB.

HISTORY:

The honey owes its characteristics to its site. The Chelsea Physic Garden was established in the late seventeenth century on about 4 acres (2 hectares) of land beside the River Thames in Chelsea to grow herbs for medical purposes and teach their identification and use to physicians and apothecaries. It flourished through the eighteenth century under the direction of some very distinguished gardeners but was neglected by the early 1900s. It was rescued from decline and used until the 1980s for teaching purposes; it then became an independent charity and was opened to the public. Still functioning as a research centre, it is a rare example of an urban garden which exists for more than ornamental purposes and is an ideal place in which to uphold the tradition of urban beekeeping which has existed for many years in Britain. Amateur beekeepers (of which there are a large number in the UK) recognize that bees kept in towns produce good yields of honey, because they can exploit the wide range of ornamental flowering plants cultivated by city gardeners to give colour through the year.

TECHNIQUE:

The garden occupies a well-drained, sheltered, south-facing site in central London. About 6,000 species are represented. The area immediately round is also rich in mixed flowers and shrubs, some of which inevitably are worked by the bees. A number of hives are kept in the garden all year; they remain in one place, carefully sited to keep the main flight-lines out of the paths of the visiting public. Swarms are prevented by removing extra queens so that only one remains in each hive. The honey is removed in late July, extracted from the comb by conventional methods, and bottled.

REGION OF PRODUCTION:

SOUTH EAST ENGLAND, LONDON.

Cumberland Sauce

DESCRIPTION:

CUMBERLAND SAUCE IS DARK RED AND TRANSLUCENT; SOME TYPES HAVE MUSTARD GRAINS VISIBLE. THE FLAVOUR IS SWEET-SOUR, REDOLENT OF SPICED FRUIT.

HISTORY:

The history of this sauce is obscure. It appears to have little to do with Cumberland. 'Oxford Sauce' is a similar recipe but has not been commercialized. The ingredients point towards origins in British cookery after 1700, when each of them was popular as accompaniment or flavouring for meat dishes. The sauce is eaten with ham, tongue, game or other cold meats.

Elizabeth David (1970) quoted a legend that the sauce was named for Ernest, Duke of Cumberland, brother of George IV. She suggests that it may have been German in origin, and observes that, 'it is odd that no recipe for Cumberland sauce as such appears in any of the nineteenth-century standard cookery books'. The first recipe for a sauce of this type is given by chef Alexis Soyer in 1853, and the first one specifically named Cumberland was given by Suzanne in *La Cuisine Anglaise* early in the 1900s. The earliest use of the name in a literary context is 1878, mentioning its use with game (*OED*). The recipe was confined to the home kitchen until after 1939–45 when the development of a market in speciality foods and the availability of affordable technology combined to see it manufactured and bottled by several small companies.

TECHNIQUE:

Recipes all contain red currant jelly, port wine, mustard and orange, which should be in the form of zest. It is extremely simple to make: the ingredients are gently heated together to form a smooth mixture, then bottled. A gelling agent is usually included in commercial varieties; this may be pectin, or, in cheaper types, cornstarch, which must be gelatinized before the sauce is bottled.

REGION OF PRODUCTION:

SOUTH EAST ENGLAND.

Mushroom Ketchup

DESCRIPTION:

MUSHROOM KETCHUP IS A DARK BROWN, THIN, CLEAR LIQUID. ITS FLAVOUR IS SALTY (SALT CONTENT IS ABOUT 12 PER CENT), WITH MUSHROOM AND SPICES.

HISTORY:

The word ketchup is thought to derive from a word in the Amoy dialect of Chinese denoting a brine of pickled fish. It began to appear in English cookery books in the mid-eighteenth century. Whether the recipes were influenced by Chinese methods or whether a fashionable new word was used for pre-existing recipes for spiced pickles is not clear. Mrs Glasse (1747) recognizes two things about ketchup: keeping qualities and foreign connections. One recipe, in a section addressed to 'Captains of Ships' is entitled 'To make Ketchup to keep Twenty Years'. In another, she observes that if a pint of ketchup is added to a pint of mum (a type of ale) 'it will taste like foreign ketchup'. An early recipe from Mrs Harrison (1748) entitled 'Kitchup or Mushroom Juice' suggests the word still needed explanation.

By the early nineteenth century ketchups were well-known, some based on elderberries, walnuts, lemons, or cockles but the most common was mushroom. Mrs Rundell (1806) gave 2 recipes using mushrooms. One requires the mushrooms to be salted and fermented, the liquid produced boiled with spices, bottled and sealed for 3 months, then strained and re-boiled with fresh spices, and bottled for keeping. What was often a domestic production (in the same way as anchovy sauce, above) was soon commercialized. The company of Geo. Watkins, under which brand mushroom ketchup is still made today, claims to have been established in 1830. The sauce is even now presented in a bottle of characteristically Victorian shape. Eliza Acton (1845) wrote that sauces of the ketchup kind could be bought and some of them were excellent. She also gives a recipe for 'tomata catsup', the first known reference to this sauce in English yet which has now almost annexed the word to itself alone.

TECHNIQUE:

Mushrooms are brined (5 parts mushrooms to 1 part salt) for several days. They are simmered for about 2 hours. Soy sauce, spices (typically ginger, cloves, pimento and black pepper) are added; the mixture is strained and bottled.

REGION OF PRODUCTION:

SOUTH EAST ENGLAND.

The South

South and South East England

Address Book

Trade Associations and Interest Groups

ASPARAGUS GROWERS ASSOCIATON www.british-asparagus.co.uk
ASSOCIATION OF MASTER BAKERS www.masterbakers.co.uk
ASSOCIATION OF SCOTTISH SHELLFISH GROWERS www.assg.co.uk
BEE FARMERS ASSOCIATION www.beefarmers.co.uk
BISCUIT, CAKE, CHOCOLATE AND CONFECTIONARY ALLIANCE
www.bcca.org.
BRAMLEY APPLE INFORMATION SERVICE www.bramleyapples.co.uk
BEE KEEPERS ASSOCIATION www.bbka.org.uk
BRITISH CARROT GROWERS ASSOCIATION www.bcga.info
BRITISH CHEESE BOARD www.cheeseboard.co.uk
BRITISH DEER FARMERS ASSOCIATION www.bdfa.co.uk
BRITISH GOOSE PRODUCERS ASSOCIATION www.goose.cc
BRITISH HERB TRADE ASSOCIATION www.bhta.org.uk
BRITISH PIG ASSOCIATION www.britishpigs.co.uk
BRITISH SUMMER FRUITS www.britishsummerfruits.co.uk
BRITISH SOFT DRINKS ASSOCIATION www.britishsoftdrinks.com
BRITISH WATERFOWL ASSOCIATION www.waterfowl.org.uk
BROGDALE HORTICULTURAL TRUST www.brogdale.org
CAMPAIGN FOR REAL ALE www.camra.org.uk
CARROT GROWERS ASSOCIATION www.bcga.info

COMMON GROUND www.england-in-particular.info
CURRY CLUB www.thecurryclub.org.uk
DAIRY TRADE FEDERATION www.dairyuk.org
ENGLISH APPLES AND PEARS www.englishapplesandpears.co.uk
ENGLISH FARM CIDER CENTRE www.middlefarm.com
FOOD FROM BRITAIN www.foodfrombritain.co.uk
FOOD AND DRINK FEDERATION www.fdf.org.uk
GAME CONSERVANCY TRUST www.gct.org.uk
GIN AND VODKA ASSOCIATION OF GREAT BRITAIN
www.ginvodka.org
GUILD OF Q BUTCHERS www.guildofqbutchers.com
HENRY DOUBLEDAY RESEARCH ASSOCIATION
(ORGANIC GARDENING AND FOOD) www.gardenorganic.org.uk
HERB SOCIETY www.herbsociety.co.uk
KENTISH COBNUTS ASSOCIATION
www.kentishcobnutsassciation.co.uk
MEAT AND LIVESTOCK COMMISSION www.mlc.org.uk
NATIONAL FRUIT COLLECTION www.webvalley.co.uk
NATIONAL ASSOCIATION OF CIDER MAKERS www.cideruk.com
NATIONAL FARMERS UNION www.nfuonline.com
NATIONAL FEDERATION OF WOMEN'S INSTITUTES
www.womens-institute.co.uk
NATIONAL MARKET TRADERS FEDERATION www.nmtf.co.uk
NATIONAL SHEEP ASSOCIATION www.nationalsheep.org.uk
QUALITY MEAT SCOTLAND www.qmscotland.co.uk
RARE BREEDS SURVIVAL TRUST www.rbst.org.uk
SAUSAGE APPRECIATION SOCIETY www.sausagefans.com
SCOTCH MALT WHISKY SOCIETY www.smws.com
SCOTTISH ASSOCIATION OF MASTER BAKERS www.samb.co.uk
SCOTTISH ASSOCIATION OF MEAT WHOLESALERS
www.scottish-meat-wholesalers.org.uk
SCOTTISH CROP RESEARCH INSTITUTE www.scri.sari.ac.uk

SCOTTISH FEDERATION OF MEAT TRADERS ASSOCIATION
www.sfmta.co.uk

SCOTTISH QUALITY SALMON www.scottishsalmon.co.uk

SEA FISH INDUSTRY AUTHORITY www.seafish.org.uk

SEASONING AND SPICE ASSOCIATION (UK)
www.seasoningandspice.org.uk

SHELLFISH ASSOCIATION OF GREAT BRITAIN www.shellfish.org.uk

SOIL ASSOCIATION www.soilassociation.org

SOUTH-WEST OF ENGLAND CIDER MAKERS ASSOCIATION
http://tinyurl.com/pylmg

SPECIALIST CHEESEMAKERS ASSOCIATION
www.specialistcheesemakers.co.uk

TASTE OF SHROPSHIRE www.shropshiretourism.info/food-and-drink/

TASTE OF THE WEST www.tasteofthewest.co.uk

TASTE OF WALES LTD www.wela.co.uk

TASTES OF ANGLIA LTD www.tastesofanglia.com

THREE COUNTIES CIDER AND PERRY ASSOCIATION
www.thethreecountiesciderandperryassociation.co.uk

TRADITIONAL FARM FRESH TURKEY ASSOCIATION
www.golden-promise.co.uk

UK TEA COUNCIL www.teacouncil.co.uk

UNITED KINGDOM VINEYARDS ASSOCIATION
www.englishwineproducers.com

WATERCRESS GROWERS ASSOCIATION www.watercress.co.uk

WINE AND SPIRIT TRADE ASSOCIATION www.wsta.co.uk

PRODUCERS, SUPPLIERS AND PARTICULAR INTEREST GROUPS
This is by no means an exhaustive list, but this list will point readers wishing to sample a taste of Britain in the right direction. Where possible, a website is given. For smaller organizations or individuals without a functioning website, a postal address is given.

The address book echoes the structure of the text, organized into categories that roughly reflect the natural order of a visit to market: fruit and vegetables, dairy, fishmonger, butchery, bakery, confectioners, drinks and condiments.

Fruit

BLENHEIM ORANGE apple
Sepham Farm, Filston Lane, Shoreham, Kent TN14 5JT.
BLUEBERRY (HIGH BUSH)
Trehane Blueberries http://tinyurl.com/pazyv
Scottish Crop Research Institute, (SCRI), Invergowrie, Dundee DD2 5DA.
STRAWBERRY
Darby Brothers, Darby Bros Farms Ltd, Bam's Hall Farm, West Dereham, Kings Lynn, Norfolk PE33 3RP.
Hugh Lowe Farms www.hlf.co.uk

Dairy Produce

CHEESE

CAROLINA CHEESE
Nepicar Farm www.nepicarfarm.co.uk

SUSSEX SLIPCOTE CHEESE
Sussex High Weald Dairy www.highwealddairy.co.uk

WELLINGTON CHEESE
Village Maid Cheeses, The Cottage, Basingstoke Road, Riseley,
Reading, Berkshire RG7 1QD.

Fish & Seafood

OYSTER
Colchester Oyster Fishery Ltd. www.colchesteroysterfishery.com

PATUM PEPERIUM
Elsenham Quality Foods Ltd, Bishop's Stortford,
Hertfordshire CM22 6DT.

SEASALTER SHELL www.seacaps.com

SMOKED SPRAT
Butley Orford Oysterage www.butleyorfordoysterage.co.uk

SMOKED SALMON (LONDON CURE)
H. Forman and Son www.formans.co.uk

YARMOUTH BLOATER
The Lowestoft Laboratory, Centre for Environment, Fisheries
and Aquaculture Science www.cefas.co.uk

Meat

Cattle
Sussex cattle
The Sussex Cattle Society www.sussexcattlesociety.org.uk

Sheep
Romney sheep
Romney Sheep Breeders Society www.romneysheepuk.co.uk
Southdown sheep
The Southdown Sheep Society www.southdownsheepsociety.co.uk

Pigs
Berkshire pig
The Berkshire Breeder's Club www.berkshirepigs.co.uk

Poultry
Aylesbury duck
R. Waller, Long Grove Wood Farm, 234 Chartridge Lane, Chesham, Buckinghamshire HP5 2SG.
Norfolk Black turkey
Kelly Turkey Farms www.kelly-turkeys.com

Meat Products

Bedfordshire clanger
Gunns Bakers, 8 Market Square, Sandy, Bedfordshire.
Oxford sausage
Stroff's, 96 Covered Market, Oxford OX1 3DY.

Breads

Kentish huffkins
The Baker's Oven www.bakersoven.co.uk

Cakes & Pies

Cider cake
R. Peel, Berryhill Farm, Coedkernew, Newport, Gwent NP10 8UD.
Suffolk Larder www.suffolklarder.co.uk
Maids of honour
Newens Bakers, The Original Maids of Honour, 288 Kew Road,
Kew Gardens, Surrey TW9 3DU.

Confectionery

Bittermints
Bendicks of Mayfair Ltd www.bendicks.co.uk

Aromatics & Condiments

Chelsea Physic Garden honey
The Chelsea Physic Garden www.chelseaphysicgarden.co.uk
Cumberland sauce
The Tracklement Co Ltd www.tracklement.co.uk
Mushroom ketchup
Peter Mushrooms www.petermushrooms.co.uk

Beverages

APPLE JUICE

Hebling, The Ruffett Duskin Farm, Covert Lane, Kingston, Canterbury, Kent CT4 6JS.

BARLEY WINE

Young's www.youngs.co.uk

BITTER BEER (KENT)

Shepherd Neame Ltd www.shepherd-neame.co.uk

P. and D.J. Goacher, Unit 8, Tovil Green Business Park, Tovil, Maidstone, Kent ME15 6TA.

ELDERFOWER CORDIAL

Belvoir Fruit Farms www.belvoirfruitfarms.co.uk

Bottlegreen www.bottle-green.co.uk

Thorncroft www.thorncroftdrinks.co.uk

The Original Drinks Co. www.originaldrinks.com

Larkins Brewery Ltd, Larkins Farm Hampkins Hill Road, Chiddingstone, Edenbridge, Kent TN8 7BB.

IMPERIAL RUSSIAN STOUT

Courage Ltd, John Smith's Brewery, Tadcaster, North Yorkshire LS24 9SA.

SAMUEL SMITH'S OLD BREWERY

www.merchantduvin.com/pages/5_breweries/samsmith.html

McMullen & Sons Ltd www.mcmullens.co.uk

SLOE GIN

Gordon's Gin www.gordons-gin.co.uk

PGOs and PGIs

Britain and continental Europe possess an enormous range of wonderful food. When a product's reputation extends beyond national borders, however, it can find itself in competition with products using the same name and passing themselves off as genuine. This unfair competition discourages producers and misleads consumers, and for this reason the European Union in 1992 created systems known as Protected Designation of Origin and Protected Geographical Indication to promote and protect regionally important food products. A Protected Designation of Origin (PDO) describes a food that is produced, processed and prepared in a given geographical area, using a recognised skill. A Protected Geographical Indication (PGI) demonstrates a geographical link between a foodstuff and a specific region in at least one of the stages of production, processing or preparation.

For more information, visit

http://ec.europa.eu/agriculture/qual/en/uk_en.htm

Bibliography

Unless otherwise indicated, the place of publication is London and the country of publication is the United Kingdom.

Acton, Eliza (1845), *Modern Cookery for Private Families*, facsimile ed., introduction by Elizabeth Ray, 1993, Southover Press, Lewes.

Austen, Jane (1995), *Jane Austen's Letters, ed. D. Le Faye*, Oxford.

Ayrton, Elizabeth (1975), *The Cookery of England*, André Deutsch.

———— (1980), *English Provincial Cooking*, Mitchell Beazley.

Beeton, Isabella (1861), *Beeton's Book of Household Management*, facsimile ed. 1982, Chancellor Press.

Borrow, George (1862), *Wild Wales*.

Boyd, Lizzie (1976), *British Cookery*, Croom Helm, Bromley.

Bradley, Martha (1756), *The British Housewife*, facsimile ed. 1997-8, Prospect Books, Totnes.

Bradley, Richard (1736), *The Country Housewife and Lady's Director*, ed. Caroline Davidson, 1982, Prospect Books.

Brown, M. (1986), 'Cider Making in the Channel Isles', Folk Life, vol. 25.

Cassell's (1896), *Cassell's Dictionary of Cookery* (first ed. c. 1875).

Cox, J. Stevens (1971), *Guernsey Dishes of Bygone Days, St Peter Port*, Guernsey.

Dallas, E.S. (1877), *Kettner's Book of The Table*, facsimile ed.1968, Centaur Press.

David, Elizabeth(1977), *English Bread and Yeast Cookery*, Allen Lane.

Davidson, Alan E. (1979) *North Atlantic Seafood*, Macmillan.

———— (1988) *Seafood, A Connoisseur's Guide and Cookbook*, Mitchell Beazley.

———— (1991), *Fruit*, Mitchell Beazley.

———— (1993) 'Sherbets', Liquid Nourishment, ed. C.A. Wilson, Edinburgh University Press.

Davies, S. (1993), 'Vinetum Britannicum, Cider and Perry in the seventeenth century', Liquid Nourishment, ed. C.A. Wilson, Edinburgh University Press.

'Dods, Meg' ['Dods, Mrs Margaret, of the Cleikum Inn, St Ronan's'] (1826), The Cook and House-wife's Manual, Edinburgh. (Written anonymously by Christian Isobel Johnstone.)

Edlin, A. (1805), *A Treatise on the Art of Breadmaking*, reprinted 1992, Prospect Books, Totnes.

Evans, J. (1994), *The Good Beer Guide* (1995), CAMRA Books, St Albans.

Evelyn, John (1699), *Acetaria. A Discourse of Sallets*, new edition, 1996, Prospect Books, Totnes.

Farley, John (1783), *The London Art of Cookery*.

FitzGibbon, Theodora (1965), *The Art of British Cooking*, Phoenix House.

Freeman, Bobby (1980), *First Catch Your Peacock*, Image Imprint, Griff thstown.

French, R.K. (1982), *The History and Virtues of Cyder*, Robert Hale.

Gerard, John (1597), *The Herball*.

Glasse, Hannah (1747), *The Art of Cookery Made Plain and Easy*, facsimile 1983, Prospect Books.

Grigson, Jane(1984), *Observer Guide to British Cookery*, Michael Joseph.

Hall, S.J.G. and Clutton-Brock, J. (1989), *Two Hundred Years of British Farm Livestock*, British Museum.

Hartley, Dorothy (1954), *Food in England*, Macdonald and Janes.

Hogan, W. (1978), *The Complete Book of Bacon*, Northwood Publications.

Irons, J.R. (c. 1935), *Breadcraft*, privately published.

Jackson, Michael (1989), *Malt Whisky Companion*, Dorling Kindersley.

—— (1993), *Michael Jackson's Beer Companion*, Mitchell Beazley.

Jenkins, J,G. (1971), 'Commercial Salmon Fishing in Welsh Rivers', Folk Life, vol. 9.

—— (1977), 'Cockles and Mussels, aspects of shellfish gathering in South Wales', Folk Life, vol. 15.

Jesse, J.H. (1901), *George Selwyn and his Contemporaries*, Nimmo.

Kirkland, J. (1907), *The Modern Baker*, Confectioner and Caterer, Gresham Publishing Company.

Kitchiner, W. (1817), *The Cook's Oracle* (1829 ed.) Larousse Gastronomique (1938), Paris.

Mabey, David (1978), *In Search of Food, traditional eating and drinking in Britain*, Macdonald and Jane's.

Mars, Valerie (1998), 'Little Fish and Large Appetites', *Fish, Food from the Waters*, Oxford Symposium on Food and Cookery, ed. Harlan Walker, Prospect Books, Totnes.

Marshall, Mrs A.B. (1887), *Mrs A.B. Marshall's Cookery Book*, 1st ed. (n.d.)

Marshall, M.W. (1987), *Fishing, the coastal tradition*, BT Batsford Ltd.

Martin, C. (1993), *Our Daily Bread*, Tabb House, Padstow.

Mayhew, Henry (1861), *London Labour and the London Poor*.

Morgan, Joan and Richards, Alison (1993), *A Book of Apples*, Ebury Press.

Murrell, John (1638), *Murrels Two books of Cookerie and Carving 1638*, facsimile ed.1985, Jackson's of Ilkley.

Neild, Robert (1995), *The English, the French and the Oyster*, Quiller Press.

Nott, J. (1726), *Cook's and Confectioner's Dictionary*, facsimile ed. 1980, Lawrence Rivington.

Penrose, John (1983), *Letters from Bath, 1766–1767*, ed.

Poulson, J. (1978), *Lakeland Recipes Old and New*, Countryside Publications, Chorley.

Raffael, Michael(1997), *West Country Cooking, Baking*, Halsgrove, Tiverton.

Raffald, E. (1769), *The Experienced English Housekeeper*, facsimile of 1782 ed. 1970, E&W Books.

Rance, Patrick (1982), *The Great British Cheese Book*, Macmillan.

Roach, F.A. (1985), *Cultivated Fruits of Britain*, Basil Blackwell, Oxford.

Rundell, Maria Eliza (1807), *A New System of Domestic Cookery*, by a Lady.

Schnebbelie, J.C. (1804), *The Housekeeper's Instructor* by W.A. Henderson, corrected revised and considerably improved by Jacob Christopher Schnebbelie.

Simon, A.L. (1960), *The Concise Encyclopaedia of Gastronomy*, Collins (1983 ed., Penguin Books).

Skuse, E. (c. 1892), *The Confectioner's Handbook*.

Spencer, Colin (1994), 'The Magical Samphire', *Disappearing Foods*, Oxford Symposium on Food and Cookery, ed. Harlan Walker, Prospect Books, Totnes.

Spicer, D.G. (1949), *From an English Oven*, The Women's Press, New York, USA.

Stobart, Tom (1980), *The Cook's Encyclopaedia*, Batsford.

Tee, George (1983), 'Samphire', *Petits Propos Culinaires* 15.

Thompson, Flora (1939), *Lark Rise to Candleford*, Guild Books.

Tibbott, Minwel (1976), *Welsh Fare*, The National Museum of Wales, Cardiff.

Webb, Mrs A. (c. 1930), *Farmhouse Cookery*, George Newnes.

White, Florence (1932), *Good Things in England*, Jonathan Cape.

Wilson, C. Anne (1973), *Food and Drink in Britain*, Constable.

Wright, Joseph (1896–1905), *The English Dialect Dictionary*, Henry Frowde.

Youatt, W. (1834), *Cattle*.

'One can say everything best over a meal.'
GEORGE ELIOT, ADAM BEDE